Sharing her own story with incredible honesty, Julie Barnhill has written a book that truly can assist mothers everywhere. *She's Gonna Blow!* gives hope and help to women struggling with anger. What an excellent resource for those who desire to grow in their relationship with God and their family!

—Jill Savage
Founder and National Director, Hearts at Home

With liberal doses of humor, Julie Barnhill points you to God's grace as the means to help prepare, repair, and tame angry hearts and behaviors. Whether you've just thought about getting mad, blown your yelling cork completely, or acted out in inappropriate ways, *She's Gonna Blow!* offers hope, understanding, and good measures of laughter and wise counsel.

—Charlene Ann Baumbich
Author of *Don't Miss Your Kids* and *365 Ways to Connect With Your Kids*

Finally! An honest book that allows us to admit out loud that there are times when all of us have blown it as mothers! Julie Barnhill writes with wit and humor of her own experience as a mother who loves her children but is often infuriated by their behavior. Entertaining, challenging, and life-changing, *She's Gonna Blow!* is destined to be a parenting classic!

—Carol Kent
President, Speak Up Speaker Services

When it comes to mothers who explode, Julie Barnhill has been there and is courageous enough to talk about it. More importantly, she has learned from her journey, and so will you. I predict you'll laugh, you'll cry, and you'll identify with Julie's open, honest approach to mothers and anger.

—Gary D. Chapman, Ph.D.
Author of *The Five Love Languages of Children*

To every mother who's ever blown it, yelled when she should have sent herself to time-out, and wants to believe she can change—this is the book for you. If you've ever sighed and cried after you've lost it with your kids (who hasn't?) and wondered if there's a way to raise children and still keep your mind, Julie Barnhill is the friend indeed that your heart needs. She points the way out of the maze of mothering madness with hilarity, empathy, and spiritual wisdom. Read This Book: Your kids will thank you!

—Becky Freeman
National speaker and author of *Worms in My Tea,*
Peanut Butter Kisses & Mud Pie Hugs, **and** *Coffee Cup*
Friendship & Cheesecake Fun

I relate to everything Julie Barnhill writes about because I also took out my anger on my children many years ago. I wish I could have had her book then because I know it could have helped me become the loving mom I wanted to be much faster than I did. If you're struggling with frustration toward your children, no matter to what degree, breathe a sigh of relief instead of blowing your top! You're about to get the help and encouragement you need so that you won't blow again!

—Kathy Collard Miller
Speaker and author of
Why Do I Put So Much Pressure on Myself?

She's Gonna BLOW!

Julie Ann Barnhill

HARVEST HOUSE PUBLISHERS
Eugene, Oregon 97402

Cover by Terry Dugan and Associates, Minneapolis, Minnesota

SHE'S GONNA BLOW!
Copyright © 2001 by Julie Ann Barnhill
Published by Harvest House Publishers
Eugene, Oregon 97402

Barnhill, Julie Ann, 1965-
    She's gonna blow! / Julie Ann Barnhill.
        p. cm.
    ISBN 0-7369-0433-6
    1. Parenting. 2. Anger. I. Title.

HQ755.8 .B377 2001
649'.1—dc21   00-059759

Printed in the United States of America.

02 03 04 05 / RDP-MS / 10 9 8 7 6 5

Contents

Appendixes: Help, Resources, and Information

—For Rick—

You love me with a single-mindedness
that still catches me off guard.
I could not have done this without your
love, devotion, and unswerving commitment
to me, our children, and the hurting moms
who needed to hear this message.
I love you.

"This is my beloved and this is my friend."
—Song of Solomon 5:16

You Have Never Been Alone

The room was filled with three or four hundred women. Noisy chatter and punctuating laughter filled the lecture hall as I waited nervously to begin the first-ever presentation of "She's Gonna Blow!" The place was Bloomington, Illinois, and it was the annual spring conference of Hearts at Home, an organization that supports mothers and mothering.

Trusting the recommendation of popular keynote speaker Charlene Ann Baumbich, Hearts at Home extended an invitation to me, a relative no-name (my mom knew me!), and gave me the opportunity of a lifetime. I told Dee Kirwan, the workshop coordinator, that I would be content speaking in a broom closet! What a tremendous opportunity this was going to be!

Over the next few months, I prayed that God would draw the very women that needed to hear the message and the heart of my presentation. I prayed that my outline would be clear and would provide the things these mothers longed to hear.

I prayed that at least 12 ladies would sign up.

About three weeks before the conference date, I received a phone call from the director of Hearts at Home,* Jill Savage. As soon as she identified herself, my heart sank.

Oh no, I thought. *She's going to cancel the workshop because of lack of interest. There are probably not enough moms to fill the broom closet.*

Of course, Jill knew nothing of the conversation I was having with myself as she began to speak.

"Julie, I wanted to call you personally and let you know something about your workshop…"

Yep, here it comes. I waited for the broom to drop.

"…One out of five mothers chose 'She's Gonna Blow!' as the workshop they most wanted to attend!"

Okay, there it is—wait a minute—what did she just say?

"Julie, we've never had this type of response to a workshop before. I think there are a lot of angry moms out there!"

Then she asked the question that put me over the top!

"Julie, would you mind presenting this workshop two times on Friday and Saturday?"

Would I mind? Would I mind! I quickly replied, "I'd love to," and thanked her for giving me the opportunity to speak a message I knew had an audience that was longing for hope. After our phone conversation ended, I was literally brought to my knees in thanksgiving. I knew that one out of five women had chosen "She's Gonna Blow!" not as a result of the speaker, but rather because they were drawn by a loving heavenly Father who knew their hearts intimately.

He knew that the tears, the frustrations, and the triumphs I had experienced were going to be used for eternal purposes, purposes beyond anything I had imagined or dreamed. And I now knew, beyond a shadow of a doubt, that I was not alone!

---

*See page 269 for more information about Hearts at Home.

On that cool March weekend three years ago, I found myself holding, praying with, crying with, laughing with, and encouraging mother after mother. One by one they came at the close of each session. Some weeping—and others quietly nodding their heads as they watched one another share the agony that had drawn them to this place and this seminar...

"Julie, I've never told anyone this before but..."

"Julie, sometimes I'm afraid I'm going to really hurt my two-year-old."

"Julie..." Then absolute breakdown.

"Julie, *what do I do now?*"

She's Gonna Blow!—this book—is my answer to the heart's agony of that question. There was never any doubt in my mind about the title. Those three simple words succinctly convey the magnitude of a mother's built-up frustration toward her children. They create a mental image of a mother who is *anything* but calm, cool, and collected.

Who is she? Well, you already know the answer to that one.

She's someone existing on four hours of sleep a night. Someone trying to handle a high-spirited, strong-willed child in the midst of Toys "R" Us. She's a single mom. Or a night-shift mom. Or a mother with "tween-agers." Or a stepmother. Or a mother with five children at home and one on the way. She may well be a mother who's trying to write a book on anger while homeschooling three young kids!

She's Gonna Blow! indeed! That mother sounds amazingly like you and me. In fact, if you're anything like me, *She's Already Blown It!* might be more to the point. And really, that's the whole purpose for this book. It's a practical guide for anyone who is wrestling with the down-to-earth and often infuriating realities of being a mom. It's also a loving message from a mother who's blown it more times than she can count—but who, with God's grace, is finally learning how to handle her anger better.

Now more than ever, I believe that we all benefit when someone candidly admits her battles, failures, and flat-out mistakes in the realm of mothering, as I did at that first workshop presentation. But when we tell the good and the bad—and I do mean bad—and unmask the gut-wrenching truth of what we think and how we *are* when no one is around, we do so with no guaranteed safety net of approval. There will be those who are taken aback at the harsh reality of our secrets and will find it hard to reconcile this reality with what they think they know of us. Yet, it is in these emotionally naked and vulnerable moments that we truly help others.

Trust me, girls, Julie Ann Barnhill does not take the "naked" part lightly! One of my greatest fears is to slip on a piece of toddler soap chalk while showering and be knocked unconscious. My well-trained children would make the obligatory 9-1-1 call—blatantly disregarding our family policy of "If Naked, Don't Tell"—thereby ensuring my complete and utter humiliation!

But the naked truth is this: In fits of uncontrolled anger I have acted and spoken harshly and irresponsibly toward my children and have thought even worse. In the midst of parental rage I have tried to justify what I called "discipline" when in reality I had crossed a shameful unspoken boundary. I have collapsed in despair at what I had become as a mother. Even now, when the good days outweigh the bad a hundred to one, the scars of past regrets are still sensitive and tender.

At one point in my search for answers to this anger I went to various bookstores and asked each manager to kindly direct me to the parenting section for a practical, honest book dealing with angry, irritated, regretful, and miserable mothering.

There were none.

There is now—or at least I hope so.

And it's for you—to let you know that someone else has been exactly where you are right now...or where you think you might be going. You have never been alone, though it may have seemed that way on far too many days. You have never been beyond hope for change—though you may have wondered if it was too late. The Father of all knows you, and He has seen your struggle and tears. You have never been beyond His reach, though you may believe you are unworthy of such mercy.

Read this book as a personal journal entry from me to you. Seize this moment to face your anger and find help for it. And never, never forget that He is full of compassion and lovingkindness. You've never fallen beyond the reach of His grace, and He will never let you go—even when you know you've blown it.

The LORD is compassionate and gracious,
slow to anger and abounding in lovingkindness....
He has not dealt with us according to our sins....
For as high as the heavens are above the earth,
so great is His lovingkindness toward those who fear Him.
As far as the east is from the west, so far has He
removed our transgressions from us. Just as a father
[mother] has compassion on his [her] children,
so the LORD has compassion on those who fear Him....
The lovingkindness of the LORD is from everlasting to
everlasting on those who fear Him.
—PSALM 103:8-13,17

Part One

Exploring
Mount Momma

How Did I Get Here?

Some Unwelcome Discoveries About Motherhood, Anger, and Really Blowing It

The veil was lifted for me one gorgeous Saturday morning in an Effingham, Illinois, bank lobby. That was the day I realized with 100-percent clarity, like Dorothy in the *Wizard of Oz*, that I wasn't in Kansas anymore!

I was standing in line that summer morning with about 12 other customers and my 18-month-old daughter. The lobby was bustling with customers, all waiting for over-stressed tellers who would have preferred to be out sunbathing rather than give change to yet one more customer.

The banking center had an open design that made all the "personal bankers" privy to the comings and goings of their customers. In addition, the bank managers had their offices along the perimeter of the building, each enclosed with glass walls that afforded every titled employee a front-row seat to any banking spectacles—such as the one I was about to present.

I was third in line, and little Kristen was standing directly behind me. Even 11 years later, I can still remember distinctly the clothes that she and I were wearing.

Kristen sported a cute summer outfit with a large red strawberry on the shirt and tiny baby strawberries on the matching shorts. Her silky dark brown hair fell just to her shoulders and drew up into bouncy tendrils that framed her chocolate brown eyes. Her smooth olive complexion and mischievous expression had caused more than one fellow mother to exclaim, "How adorable!"

I had delivered my second child, Ricky Neal, about three weeks before and was sporting the appropriate clothing for one who until recently had been very pregnant. My oversized T-shirt, knotted loosely at my hips, strategically camouflaged the results of carrying a nine-pound-eight-ounce bundle of joy. The black, stretchy Capri leggings accented at the calves with a wide band of lace did their best not to give away the Oreo cookie raids preceding his birth.

I might not have been quite as adorable as my toddler daughter that morning, but overall I felt pretty terrific, because I had netted $717.83 from a garage sale that previous weekend. Yes, you read that right—seven hundred seventeen dollars and eighty-three cents! I had gotten rid of the 4-H sewing machine I had used about five times since eighth grade and the dining room furniture that we had all used way too much. I had put a price tag on just about everything—even my husband Rick's unused golf clubs and useless baseball equipment from high school. If an overzealous shopper hadn't called and talked to Rick, I would have actually sold the clubs and ball equipment! Nevertheless, my home was less cluttered, and as I stood in that bank lobby, the Wal-Mart sack in my hand was weighted down with my $717.83—mostly in quarters, nickels, and pennies.

While Kristen and I waited, she entertained the captive audience with such feats as spinning around until she was dizzy, scrunching her nose and lips to make an obnoxious breathing sound through her nostrils, and making faces at the people behind us. I, of course, felt delighted to have such a cute and precocious child.

I had moved up to second in line when Kristen started to turn her attention to me. Her mother. The woman who had agonized 14 hours, surviving on ice chips alone, to bring her into this world!

She began to turn her attention, all 18 months' worth, to me. The woman who thought the sun rose and set on this child.

"Next," said the teller.

I stepped to the window and plopped my sack of dollars, quarters, nickels, and three pennies on the cold marble countertop. Teller-girl threw me a deadly look and began sorting coins.

"Oh," I volunteered brightly, "I've counted it already, and there is $717.83. I got it all from a garage sale!" I smiled, knowing she'd appreciate my attention to detail and my business prowess.

"You don't say?" She rolled her eyes and started counting, " Five, ten, fifteen…"

I glanced back to check on Kristen and then rested my elbows on the countertop, leaning forward and relaxing, just taking it easy and thinking how I was going to spend all that money.

"One hundred five, one hundred fifteen…"

This was the point where Kristen turned her full attention to me. I felt a small, tentative poke on my, er…backside.

I ignored it.

Bad decision.

Then, another small—but decidedly stronger than the first—poke against my backside, accompanied by a singsong voice proclaiming, "Big bottom, Mom! Big bottom!"

Poke, poke, prod, prod.

I whipped around and saw my three-foot munchkin grinning from ear to ear. With each prod and poke, her tiny voice grew in confidence, bolstered by smiles and chuckles from those in her immediate vicinity.

I lowered my head, unknotted my shirt, and whispered delicately, "Kristen, stop poking Mommy's bottom...and quit saying 'big bottom.' It isn't nice to talk about Mommy's bottom. Now, don't say the word *bottom* again."

I turned back to the teller, who was trying with little success to quell a smirk and count dimes accurately. Not a peep could be heard from behind me. Good.

But no, the silence following my little chat with Kristen was *not* good. Definitely not good. She had used those brief moments for thinking, and now the small poke flowered into an all-out punch. With her tiny yet accurate pointer finger aiming for the rear, Kristen proclaimed for everyone, teller and glass-ensconced manager alike, to hear:

"Big butt! Momma, big butt!" (Well, I did tell her not to say "bottom.")

Then, as I melted into a puddle of public humiliation and the teller snorted aloud with laughter, I saw the light! It all made perfect sense.

From a simple bank transaction to the ordeal of combing through laundry to find baby booties that matched, my life had been irrevocably changed—and I was the last to figure it out.

I had gone from designer size-tens to plus-size stretch pants with lace, and I was the last to get it.

Intellectual banquets of J.R.R. Tolkien and C.S. Lewis had degenerated to Spam sticks of *People* magazine and Mercer Mayer, and I was only now beginning to understand...that my life would never be the same again.

TimeOut/Tamer: Times like this are good occasions to start repeating the sane mother's creed: "This too shall pass." (It really will—no matter how you feel at the moment!)

Yes, until motherhood I had never been accosted and mortified by a three-foot-tall relation. Until motherhood, I never knew to look *forward* to winter because kids need fewer baths then. Until motherhood, I had never publicly discussed the size and shape of my uterus nor used the medical terms *adhesions* and *circumcision* in the same sentence.

This moment was only the beginning. Motherhood was to be the impetus of monumental changes in my life…and the most surprising ones began in the bathroom!

Porcelain Petitions

There I sat, chin to rim with our family commode, wedged between a cold porcelain tub and a veneer-covered vanity and shaking my head with dismay.

How did I get here? I asked myself. *Didn't I graduate with a college degree? Doesn't my resume read "Educator Extraordinaire"?* Who would have thought it?

My eyes were drawn to the answer to "How did I get here?" She was poised precariously on the edge of a chipped and chilly toilet seat. Kristen Jean Barnhill, her two-year-old legs juuust long enough to bend and clutch the bowl with her ankles, was hunched forward, lips firmly set, assessing me with an impish and determined gaze.

Note I did not say "precious" gaze.

I said "impish and determined."

Fellow sisters in mothering, I had followed the rules. I had read all the necessary and recommended mothering material. Dr. Penelope Leach (note to self: This is not pronounced Pen-a-lope) was my mentor via books. Dr. T. Barry Brazelton, Dr. James Dobson, and a host of other Wise Ones had kept me on the edge of my parenting seat.

With bated breath I had combed through each issue of *Parenting* magazine, eager to create child-pleasing culinary delights with bread, baloney, cellophane-wrapped toothpicks, and cleverly shaped cookie cutters. My VCR was set to record *American Baby* at 10:00 A.M. CST. The speed dial on my phone was programmed for 1-800-They Still Hurt.*

I had this mommy thing down to a science. I could change a diaper and effectively identify and remove cradle cap while propping a Playtex bottle for a hungry baby with my chin. Nothing could deter me from the coveted degree of Mommy Ph.D. Nothing—except…

The Number-Two Zone.

I had shelled out $697.34 for baby books over a two-year period. I had purchased every baby manual written and trusted the "professional" advice that I read. Somebody owes me a refund! Judge Judy, here I come!

Not one person, publisher, or professional ever gave the slightest hint that a two-year-old child…*the same child who couldn't find her way out of a snug turtleneck*…could voluntarily shut down all bowel action. Just like that. Here today, none tomorrow.

---

*Disclaimer: The author feels it imperative to confess that she never once experienced a La Leche, earth-mother, one-with-the-baby moment while breastfeeding child number one. She did experience one-with-the-body torment that involved her breasts and adjectives such as *engorged, cracked, infected,* and *EXCRUCIATING!* Her daughter learned to love formula, and the author does not feel guilty…much.

On this particular evening, I had stood guard at the potty for two hours. Two hours—give or take a diaper change for the baby—of earnestly imploring my darling daughter to let nature have its way.

Earnest Imploring #1: "Come on, sweetie pea, cutie-patootie, let Mr. Two take a trip to toilet land."

Response: Impish and determined.

Earnest Imploring #2: "Kristen, honey, if you do, Mommy will eventually walk upright again, and then I'll get you the biggest, best, greatest chocolate ice cream we've ever had!" (Yes, moms, that spells B-R-I-B-E-R-Y!)

Response: Impish and determined.

Earnest Imploring #3: "Precious, your friend Bailey does number two, and she's only [eyebrows raised with a "tsk-tsk" expression] one year old."

Response: Kristen pinched her eyes tightly shut, scrunched her face like a prune (a side effect from the eight glasses of said juice she had consumed with dismal results), and replied in an impish and determined voice, "But Mommy, I don't waaaaaaaaaaaaaant to."

Heavy sigh.

You know, there are a lot of things we can make our children do. We can *make* them "give your little brother a hug and say you're sorry." We can *make* them "get that look off your face!" Occasionally we can even make them happy.

However, there is no way to *force* a child to respond to nature's call if she doesn't want to, as I was discovering at that very moment.

Now, I'd like to tell you that I handled this situation in a gentle, tender, longsuffering adult fashion. After all, I was the mommy. I'd also like to tell you that I find a 12-ounce steak cooked medium rare served with salad with bleu cheese dressing and baked potato slathered in butter and sour cream unappetizing. "But mommies, I caaaaaaaaan't!"

What I did was yell.

"Kristen!" I hollered, "I'm sick of sitting here waiting for you to go to the bathroom!" I smacked her sharply on her right thigh and threatened, "Do you want a real spanking? Do you? If you don't go to the bathroom right now I will give you a spanking."

I just knew Kristen was doing this to irritate me. I knew she had to go, and I knew she was old enough to do it without such a production! The longer the two of us sat there, the angrier I became. I began to bellow on and on about the medical complications of holding in what Kristen was holding in. I stormed out of the tiny bathroom, arms waving wildly—blowing off a little steam, so to speak. Finally, I was out of steam, threats, and ravings, and I collapsed on my bed, stared at the ceiling, and let loose a high-pitched wail that indicates complete mother meltdown!

Kristen was stupefied by this most recent eruption. I was mortified that I had totally and completely lost it!

Minutes passed, and finally I returned to the scene of the crime. The 21-pound proper noun was still sitting on the seat. I placed my hands on her cheeks (*facial*, ladies) and hoarsely whispered, "Go ahead and pray, Kristen. Maybe God will help you."

As I knelt down in front of her, she raised her tiny, guilt-inducing, tear-stained face, and asked with a trembling voice and solemn, childlike faith:

"Jesus, help me poop."

You know what happened next. (Grumble, grumble... should have prayed two hours ago...grumble.) As I tucked her into bed, I kissed her repeatedly and tenderly rubbed the fading imprint of three adult fingers on her slender thigh. I brushed my hand against her forehead and pleaded with God to banish this maternal blowup from her young memory. After one last kiss and a disgusted shake of my head I asked myself, "How did I ever get here?"

What Kind of Mother Am I?

Perhaps you find yourself in the same position as I found myself. I was a mother thankful for her children but completely blindsided by the person she had become *after* motherhood. In the days, weeks, and months that followed my first two births, I scarcely recognized myself.

My journals are full of entries written before I delivered either of my first two children. I filled those pages with all my longings to hold them and to love them. I wrote of how I had prayed, even as an eight-year-old girl, that I might one day be a mother. I promised in those pages to be the greatest, most wonderful mom in the entire world.

I was going to be what every mom longs to be…"a good mother" (I know you're nodding your head in agreement here!)—

- dynamic
- involved
- compassionate
- fun
- inspiring
- loving

Honestly, I didn't have a clue.

All those grandiose pledges worked so well on paper. I could spend hours completing each profound thought and then put my pen aside and go about my pre-children activities, activities such as teaching school, reading wonderful books, and engaging in long, satisfying conversations with adults.

Then came Kristen and, 18 months later, Ricky Neal, and what I became in those brief few months wasn't even close to my original list of "good mother" adjectives. Now the list read more like—

- impatient
- discontent
- irritable
- depressed
- disappointed
- angry

Angry? Since when had I been an angry person? I had never thought of myself that way. I would get miffed or irritated or even hacked off, but angry—as in yelling, screaming, or acting out in an uncontrolled manner? Never!

Somehow between the ages of 23 and 24, I became an entirely different woman, and I didn't like it one bit.

TimeOut/Tamer: Do you find yourself assuming that you're the only mother struggling with anger toward your children? The mother you least expect may be burdened with the most secrets of anger and rage. Make a point of *really listening* to the mothers around you, and reach out to them. You never know—you may be the lifesaver that someone has been praying for—and you'll find comfort in knowing you're not the only one.

Not Alone

I remember attending a women's Bible study when my children were young and the issue of my own anger was heavy on my heart. I went there that day with a sense of anticipation and relief. What better place to find understanding and help than in a gathering of other Christian mothers? So during the prayer request time, I took a deep breath and unloaded!

I told the women, who knew me well and whom I considered to be close friends, of my frequent anger and frustration toward Ricky and Kristen. I told them how I had debated with myself that very morning about dropping my kids off for child care and just driving far, far away in my van for a long, long, long period of time. I told them I was afraid of what I might do if I got as tired and impatient as I had the previous day.

I bared my soul that day to those sisters in Christ.

The response?

"Well…" (awkward silence) "…would anyone else like to share?"

I can smile about it now, but then…whew! I wanted to curl up and die—which at the time, I might add, sounded more appealing than returning home alone with two small children!

So many of us have been there or are there right now. While I was preparing this book, in the space of two weeks *eight* women asked to read the rough draft! They wanted answers at that moment or at least wanted to commiserate with someone who understood.

I've read and reread hundreds of handwritten letters, e-mails, and hastily scribbled notes that mothers have sent me since I've been speaking on this topic. I've spoken long-distance with frantic mothers and have become an active participant in electronic message boards that deal specifically with children, moms, and anger management. I believe you will identify with many of their stories and perhaps hear your own voice crying out in theirs:

> I used to be a real patient person. I also worked full-time then. Three-and a-half years ago my husband got a new job 70 miles from where we lived, making three times the salary

with much better benefits, so we moved. We had a three-year-old boy (who's now six) at the time, and suddenly I was an at-home mom…just as I had always wanted. At first it was wonderful. Then hubby began working extra hours and started school, so he was rarely home. We had a baby girl (who's now two), and I started feeling very stressed about always being home with two kids and no husband around. A little over a year ago, I got violent toward my then five-year-old. I yelled and smacked him so hard he fell down. I knew I needed help and I hated what I had become.

—Anonymous

I struggle a lot with this. I come from an abusive back-ground. My mom yelled a lot and was very impatient. She neglected me and left me alone a lot. I also was whipped with a belt.

—Brenda

Our son is on this teasing kick. He takes great pleasure in getting me riled up. This may or may not be a preteen thing. I try not getting upset. He pulled it this morning real bad. I work a 12-hour shift today…and he got me so worked up this morning I didn't know how I would be able to concentrate on work.

—Carol

As a child I was sexually abused by an uncle, verbally/minor physically abused by my mother. No father or "normal" male role models. I have done the counseling, got the badge to prove it. I know all of the psychobabble and could probably run my own group for survivors. What makes me angry is that I have no parenting skills nor any idea of what a normal, healthy, parent-child relationship is.

—Anonymous

My daughter has been diagnosed with Attention Deficit Hyperactivity Disorder. I get so tired and frustrated of the same routine when dealing with her. As a single mom I feel helpless, alone, and angry. I can't change the way she is…but how I wish I could just step away from all of it!

—Terry

I just have such a hard time not yelling. I get so angry and haven't found (or to be perfectly honest, researched) good outlets for my anger. Instead I get all stressed out and miserable. I do not hit or spank my children! I am thankfully totally different than my mother! However, I do find myself to be impatient at times and I yell often. I hate getting angry.

—Aranda

Can you relate to these women? No matter what you are going through, you are not alone in this struggle with anger and how it plays out in your home and with your children. In your community, at your workplace, sitting next to you during worship, or at the park cheering beside you at the latest Little League game are countless numbers of mothers who are ashamed and frightened by their feelings of rage and their angry, uncontrolled behavior toward their children. They are caught in a hopeless cycle of blowing it and reaping the poisonous consequences of guilt, regret, and self-condemnation.

Not exactly what we signed up for, eh? I remember so vividly the loneliness and anguish of my early mothering years. I would beat myself up over the bad things I had said, done, and thought. I'd find myself pledging "I'll never," and hoping for some miracle—and before I knew it I would be at it again.

I learned the hard way that I was fully capable of exploding in fury and anger. It was at the expense of my children's early years that I finally came to a point of self-examination and hit upon the concept of my anger resembling a volcanic eruption...Mount Momma.

Real Mom Points to Ponder

1. Have you experienced an "aha!" moment of mothering? Where did it take place and who was involved? What is the most surprising fact you have learned about yourself since becoming a mother?

2. What parenting issues tend to be trigger points for your particular kind of anger? Under what particular circumstances do you tend to "lose it"?

3. How did you tend to communicate your feelings of anger *before* children—verbally? physically? through withdrawal or silence? Has your "anger style" changed since becoming a mother? Is the intensity level lower or higher?

4. What childhood or early adulthood ideal of "good" mothering have you regretted giving up the most? (Examples: being able to stay home full-time, successfully juggling work and family, being a "crafty" mom, *enjoying* the infant stage of children.) Stop and consider how much influence these resentments are playing out in your anger toward your children.

5. Name two moms you know who seem to be struggling with anger toward their kids. How could you use this

book as a tool to develop creative conversations and encourage one another towards change?

6. Are you harboring any secrets in regard to your anger and your behavior—things you do and feel when no one is around? Three years ago, after reading an interview I gave a local newspaper regarding anger and motherhood, my father-in-law called and asked my husband if I had been misquoted. He couldn't believe I admitted, "Yes, I acted abusively toward my children." I had hidden my explosive blowups well—even from the eyes of my in-laws. Who would have a difficult time believing your story of anger?

Volcanoes 101

Understanding How She Blows

Imagine a peaceful countryside nestled in the shadow of a majestic mountain. Crops flourish on her slopes, growing abundant in her fertile soil. Neighbors look up to her and comment on her beauty. Her head is crowned with wisps of clouds. Her very presence is a benediction.

Unfortunately, that's not the whole story—at least not when that lovely mountain is also a volcano. For such a mountain can easily appear pristine and peaceful when in fact there is an enormous cauldron of fiery rock roiling under the surface, out of sight. Slowly, over a period of months and years, the magma rises. Finally the pressure builds to such a level that something's got to give. Cinders and ash spew forth, poisonous gases fill the air, and liquid magma—or lava, as it is referred to after an eruption—rains down upon the unsuspecting and unprepared victims.

A volcano, in essence, is a natural thing that explodes under pressure. And that's exactly what can happen to us when motherhood gets to be just too much for us. In an instant we can change from the peaceful, nourishing women we want to be into Mount Momma—spitting fire and brimstone at all who cross our path.

As mothers, our levels of exploding vary. Some eruptions are relatively mild and do little harm, at least on the surface. Others—well, you've heard of Mount St. Helens, haven't you? (If you haven't, you will before this chapter is over!)

In the following paragraphs I'd like to introduce you to four types of volcanic eruptions that I believe also apply to our Mount Momma blowups. These volcanic definitions will help you identify your most common style of expressing anger toward your children.

Bear in mind, these have been chosen in order to give you a *broad* understanding of the anger in your life, its buildup, and its explosive power. Your actual experience may fit into more than one category or may feel different than any of the four. (Not all volcanoes fit into these four categories, either!) But these will help you begin considering in greater depth the specifics of how your anger builds and what actually happens in your home during the heat of anger and rage.

If you were a real volcano, what would your eruptions look like?

The Strombolian

A Strombolian eruption is named after the tiny volcanic island of Stromboli between the island of Sicily and the "boot" of Italy. Volcanic activity on this island has remained more or less the same for centuries. When the volcano "blows," its eruptions sound a lot like the din of a powerful jet engine at close range, and it spits out volcanic materials such as cinders and thick, pasty lava bombs.[1] But because the eruptions are relatively short and happen at predictable intervals, the Strombolian would seem to be one of the least threatening volcanic eruptions. After all, how much damage can a few cinders do?

To answer that, I have to ask whether you remember the episode of *Little House on the Prairie* when Albert caused a fire at a children's boarding home. He had been smoking a pipe in the cellar of the home, and when he heard approaching footsteps he attempted to hide the evidence beneath a pile of rubbish.

Remember?

He *thought* he had extinguished the pipe, and he *thought* his secret was safe. He thought wrong. Unbeknownst to Albert, tiny cinders remained in the hot ash. Minute after minute, those tiny cinders smoldered. Hour by hour they spread, until a flame sprang up and an irreparable chain of events was ignited. By the show's conclusion, two lives had been lost, and Albert had to shoulder the crushing knowledge that he was responsible.

What a tragedy—and it all began with a few cinders.

I was a Strombolian mom in my early years of parenting. Like those of Old Faithful, my eruptions were predictable, short-lived, and *seemed* to blow over with little residual damage.

I would later learn, however, that the spewing cinders of my anger could be as damaging as a blowtorch. Verbal cinders of sarcasm—such as "Yeah, right, Einstein!" and "I'm *so* glad I had kids!"—smoldered in my children's young hearts. And cinders of regret—the longing to be able to take back words and thoughts—seared my conscience in the deep of night.

What a miserable time! I would get to the end of the day and realize I hadn't laughed, relaxed, or enjoyed my children. All I had done was the same stuff I had done the day before, which I had vowed—just the day before—that I

would *never* do again. Small eruption followed small eruption...and the cumulative damage was real.

If you are a Strombolian erupter, you may have battled
with yourself while reading the last few paragraphs. *Well,
I think she's going a little overboard*, you may think. *Sure, I get
mad sometimes—but it blows over fast. It's just the way I am. My
kids know how to deal with it.*

Well, that really may be true for you, but I know it wasn't
true for me. I learned that repeated small eruptions and
cinder showers can eventually bring about as much damage
as any other kind of eruption.

TimeOut/Tamers: Sometimes you can short-circuit a volcanic explosion by concentrating on your physical reactions.
Remind yourself to breathe deeply and slowly, concentrating
on the flow of air in and out of your lungs. Consciously relax
your facial muscles—unclench your jaw and teeth, raise your
eyebrows to smooth out your forehead, unpurse your mouth.
Deliberately stretch out your hands (which may be clenched
into fists) and roll your shoulders to relax your neck. By
changing your physical response to anger, you may be able to
cool down your emotional response as well.

The Hawaiian

This is the kind of eruption they show a lot on the Discovery
Channel—partly because it's relatively easy to get television
cameras close to. Hawaiian volcanoes such as Mauna Loa
and Kilauea Iki on the island of Hawaii are mainly charac-
terized by lakes and rivers of constantly boiling lava. Often
this molten rock will seethe away in its crater, doing little
damage. Scientists and tourists (and television reporters)

can even fly overhead and see it. But sooner or later the fiery lava will boil up in the crater and overflow the sides, or it will break through cracks or fissures and start flowing downhill to the sea.

Even then, from a distance, the slow-moving streams of lava don't look that dangerous. Usually they move slowly enough that people can get out of their way. Often they're covered with a black, hardened crust that disguises their orange-hot intensity. But when they engulf a highway, incinerate a stand of trees, annihilate a subdivision, hit the ocean with a hissing explosion of steam, and leave behind acres of desolate black rock in place of green countryside— then their destructive nature becomes clear.

Are you the type of mom who specializes in this kind of chronic, simmering anger? You're not really the explosive type. You would *never* yell or throw things, and you don't like to think of yourself as an angry person. If you're really honest with yourself, however, you know there is a lot of turmoil bubbling inside of you all the time. You're the type whose insides twist into knots, or you often feel down or negative about life in general. But you're certainly safe for your children to be around.

Or are you?

The problem with being a Hawaiian mom (the volcano, not the state) is that human beings just weren't meant to live in a constant state of low-level turmoil. If you simmer and seethe long enough, even though you may avoid a violent explosion, sooner or later the anger and negativity inside you is going to break out. And the resulting damage may be all the greater because your anger doesn't seem all that dangerous on the surface.

Most often, the "lava flow" that results from a Hawaiian eruption will be verbal. Caustic criticism, negative assessments, unfavorable comparisons, sarcastic barbs, teasing that carries an edge, or just pessimistic pronouncements about life in general—all these forms of spoken terrorism can scorch and burn the people in their paths, even when they are presented as "constructive," "honest," or "joking." So can passive-aggressive behaviors such as "forgetting" to wash a particular outfit or abruptly canceling an outing your children were looking forward to.

The most marked characteristics of Hawaiian Mount Momma eruptions are that first, they often mask themselves as innocent remarks and actions, and second, they can go on for a *long* time. They may not be as explosive as other eruptions, but they keep on coming...just like the Mauna Loa lava flowing on and on to the sea. This kind of mom doesn't just blow and get it over with; she just keeps picking and harping. And she may do it all while protesting (or even *believing*), "I'm not mad; I'm just concerned...."

The Vulcanian

If you know the expression "blowing off a little steam," you have a good verbal description of what a Vulcanian eruption is like—except we're not talking about "a little" *anything*.

Whereas the Strombolian volcano regularly spews out cinders, and the Hawaiian constantly simmers and overflows, the Vulcanian type will seethe with pent-up molten rock, then expel blobs of "viscous" magma in a big, gassy explosion. If you could bottle viscous magma, it would be thick, sticky, and hard to pour—sort of like my Christmas fudge, but not as tasty. You can imagine what kind of energy would be needed to spew out material of that consistency through a relatively small opening.

Simply put, a Vulcanian explosion is loud, scary, and dangerous! The mountain erupts with clouds of ash-laden gas, steam, and all sorts of solid volcanic rock. The solid fragments violently ejected from the mountain are hot and deadly and will annihilate anything or anyone they come in contact with. The gases are usually poisonous. Clearly, you don't want to be around a Vulcanian eruption if you can help it!

That's certainly true of a mother who erupts in a Vulcanian style. She produces shrapnel—verbal, physical, emotional—that can shred the spirits of her children and the safety of her home. Sometimes she may actually throw things. More often, she lets loose with poisonous words and actions—insults, accusations, slaps and shakes. Her wrath is unpredictable, and she doesn't get over it quickly. In fact, a Vulcanian mom is capable of sustaining an eruption for days on end—often with her wrath aimed at a particular child.

An acquaintance of mine experienced the devastating reality of seeing herself erupt in a Vulcanian manner. I never knew this woman to explode in any other area *except* motherhood. Before children, she worked in a high-stress field and had to deal with the worst of the worst when it came to personality disorders and disruptive temperaments. She thought every button that *could* be pushed *had been* pushed. She thought all the years of dealing with hard-to-manage people would give her just the extra help she'd need for parenting.

Wrong.

She had kids, and the fragments started flying.

Fed up to *here* with her strong-willed daughter, this mother would engage in furious screaming fits, calling the girl names and saying she wished her girl had never been born. She would dig her fingers into the child's upper arm in an angry attempt to control the child's public behavior. Even then my friend knew, though she appeared to onlookers to be in control, that she was in fact out of control and hurting her child. But she didn't know how to stop—nor did she even want to.

I believe that's what distinguishes this type of eruption from the previous ones mentioned—the "don't want to stop" level of emotion. Whereas the Strombolian eruption consists more of "off the cuff" moments of madness and the Hawaiian flows from a low-level and sometimes unrecognized pool of anger, the Vulcanian finds a mother engaged in willful and increasingly harder-to-stop behavior. Reasonable, self-checking thoughts are increasingly harder for her to hear as her gassy cauldron of anger pours out upon her children.

The Plinian

Let me begin this final description with a word of encouragement. Chances are you have never experienced this type of eruption as a mother, yet you have probably read or heard a report about a mother who completely lost control of herself in anger and then found herself living with the devastating (or fatal) consequences of a Plinian eruption. Chances are you recognize the terrifying escalation of your anger and desperately want to avoid the nightmarish scenario such an eruption could bring to your life and future. May we all proceed with caution—realizing that anger culminates in such a result *rarely*, but certainly not *never*.

The Plinian is the most violent of volcanic eruptions. Everything about such an explosion is big and bad. The one thing above all that characterizes a Plinian eruption is the sheer *volume* of material ejected by the eruption and the sheer power of the explosion that throws it out. A Plinian eruption is so violent that it has the power to change a vast area.

If you are 30 or older, you most likely have an image seared in your memory relating to the cataclysmic eruption of Mount Saint Helens on May 18, 1980. It was with re-newed horror that I read personal accounts of survivors and details concerning those who did not survive from the online archives of a Washington newspaper.

> The Pandora's box of nature's fury following the Sunday morning explosion unleashed the fol-lowing: A series of mudflows raced down the two forks of the Toutle River, killing motorists, snapping a dozen or more highway bridges, sweeping away homes, cars, and large logging equipment rigs. A searing explosion ripped a fan-shaped swath out of the forest on the north-west side of the peak, killing several persons by the shock of the blast or the heat. In some areas the trees were clipped neatly at about 20 feet above the ground; in other areas not even a stump remained. The swath was eight miles long and 15 miles wide. Ash, several feet deep in areas close to the peak, was pushed as far as 500 miles to the east where it "turned day into night." One of the hardest hit was the Yakima area, but the impact is widespread. It closed airports, halted all but the more serious emergency ser-vices, triggered school closures, and became a major health concern. By mid-morning on the 18th, the ash cloud was as far east as Montana and Colorado.[2]

Fifty-seven people lost their lives as a direct result of Mount Saint Helens' blowing her top—or more accurately—her entire north side. It has been estimated that nearly 1.4 bil-lion cubic yards of ash fell over a 22,000-square-mile area.

If you had ever erupted in a Plinian manner, you would *know* it because of the terrible havoc it would have wreaked upon yourself, your children, and your relationships. You would *know* that this type of extreme, explosive anger—even though it might erupt infrequently—can easily destroy all that you hold most dear.

We're talking about *really* losing it—screaming until you're hoarse, rampaging through the house, perhaps even beating a child or saying the kinds of things that wither your heart when you think about them later. We're talking about angry explosions that cause your children to hide from you or leave the house (physically and emotionally)—explosions that leave you wondering what kind of monster you've become. Like an explosion that causes a volcanic dome to collapse, a Plinian outburst can effectively make the "central dome" of your mothering collapse.

I remember three mothers I spoke with privately at the Hearts at Home conference where I first presented this material. Each one struggled with the depth of her anger. Each one was desperate to avoid a Plinian moment in her life. Each one asked me, in aching whispered tones, "What if I lose my kids by telling someone how I really am?"

"What will happen to your children if you don't?" I responded.

How my heart breaks for them and for any of you who live with this fear in your hearts. But keep reading, because there is hope for you, too.

TimeOut/Tamers: When you find yourself growing angry, don't try to pretend to yourself that you're not. But remind yourself that being angry doesn't mean you have to act on your anger. In fact, try not to do *anything* until you've cooled down. Put *yourself* in the playpen if you have to. Or open the refrigerator door and just stand there and chill out! If you can't put some space between you and a problem—if, for example, you're alone with a two-year-old!—at least close your eyes and count to ten.

Volcanic Dangers

Volcanic eruptions are dangerous! Even the relatively "safe" Strombolian eruptions have the capacity to cause long-lasting harm, and the more violent kinds of explosions can destroy your family. Here are just a few examples of what you can damage with your angry outbursts:

- *Your children's sense of security.* Can a child truly feel secure in your love if he or she lives in fear of your erupting in a violent and out-of-control manner?

- *Your spouse's trust.* Have you explained away physical injuries or made light of the true stories your children told to Daddy? Can your marriage truly flourish if you are withholding the truth about your relationship with your children from the one God has made "flesh of your flesh?"

- *Your relationship with God.* We are not so far removed from Adam and Eve as we might believe. Our first thought and action in times of sin and wrongdoing is often to flee and hide from our Creator. Like me, you may fear that all God is going to do is remind you of yet one more time that you blew it—and therefore you find yourself disengaging from a relationship with Him.

Oh, my dear sisters in Christ! It doesn't have to be that way! Let me scream it from the top of the volcano! Let me say it loud and clear to Strombolian, Hawaiian, Vulcanian, Plinian, and every mom in between: *You are not alone, and you do not have to swim in a river of guilt, regret, and condemnation.* You are not the only mom, and you will not be the last mom, to deal with this issue of anger, rage, and emotional fury. And though Mount Momma poses a real danger to everything you hold dear…you are *not* doomed to be Mount Momma!

Listen to me: I'm doing the girlfriend hanky wave as I type—one hand typing and the left hand waving my white hanky while cheering you on!

If you are willing—and does any of us really *want* to ride this out alone any longer?—if you are willing to hear truth and deal with the details, you can find lifelong peace and change in this journey of mothering. We cannot do this alone. None of us are strong enough, disciplined enough, or courageous enough to deal with the cinders, the toxins, and the ash forever.

Strombolian moms, we must unite! No more excuses and no more whispered prayers of "please don't let them remember." No more!

Vulcanian moms—group hug, and let's support one another! Are you ready to stop the violent ejection of shrapnel in your words and actions? If that's an affirmative, give me a big ol' girlfriend wave!

Plinian moms, let's quit shoveling those tons of ash, trying to cope with the tragic aftermath of those huge blowups—or living in fear of the "big one"! Together we can help one another keep the dome intact and experience a home and spirit that is life-giving instead of explosive and toxic.

Moms, we need each other, and we need to call upon the One who knit us each together, who knows each and every idiosyncrasy about every one of us.

I want you to face the facts about yourself and your home and find lasting peace. I want you to recognize and understand your type of anger and know your triggers. I want you to know that defusing Mount Momma is not a matter of being able to keep one more promise of control, but of giving control to the One who made you and knows your mother heart as no one else does.

And then, I want you to be prepared to lovingly and honestly share the truth of your experience with the other hurting moms in your world.

Real Mom Points to Ponder

1. What is your most consistent style of erupting in anger? Does it resemble one of the four volcanoes described here, or would you describe it another way?

2. What is your greatest fear concerning your eruptive anger and your children?

3. Has there been a time when you knew, *without a doubt*, that your anger was uncontrolled, out of bounds, and potentially harmful to your children?

Warning Signs

How to Know
When You're Gonna Blow

You are traveling to the nearest store, the lone adult in a non-air-conditioned minivan. It is July 12, and your state is experiencing an unprecedented heat wave, with humidity factors off the charts! With you is a teething, drooling toddler who is harnessed (against his will) into a thrice-handed-down car seat. Because of its long-lasting dependability, this car seat exudes an obnoxious but oddly comforting essence of apple juice, hardened McDonalds' fries, and baby wipes (used ones).

While the toddler rises to the challenge of gnawing through the shoulder straps of that aromatic car seat, your eight-year-old daughter quietly leans over and breathes on her six-year-old brother. War is declared, and each child fumigates the other with rancid, forgot-to-brush-my-teeth-since-last-month tyrannosaurus breath. Your daughter leers. Your son pulls back an arm to strike.

You issue a "one time only!" warning and turn into the crammed parking lot, scanning in vain for an empty space within actual sight of the store. An errant cart waylays your vehicle, and you bite your tongue, *hard,* in an attempt to quell any inappropriate ravings.

As you proceed, you try to calculate just *how* negative your checkbook balance might be, search for Midol in the change holder, a.k.a. ash tray, and rack your brain for any forgotten casserole recipes that call for the following ingredients (the current contents of your refrigerator):

- one can of refrigerated biscuit dough
- an egg
- three "pinched-off-the-green-spots" slices of bread
- a single square of stiffened processed cheese

Just as you spy a space in the next row of the parking lot, you catch the distinct sound of sibling flesh slapping sibling flesh. You've turned to deal with the slapper and comfort the slappee, when a 32-ounce glass bottle rolls across the pavement directly in front of you! Swerving to miss it, you overcompensate a bit, sending a 96-ounce Big Freeze crashing to the floorboard and coating 17 past-due library books with a sugary mess.

The melee within your van has now reached a fever pitch, and approximately 23 seconds after issuing the "one time only!" warning to the Hatfields and McCoys in the back seat, you've had enough! Your lower left eyelid begins to twitch uncontrollably.

Bad sign.

With your left arm handling the steering, with your right arm you flail madly behind you—hoping to make a meaningful connection with anyone moving! Your children dodge each swat with youthful agility and glee. Your arm begins to cramp, and you resort to using your pointer finger as a deadly weapon. With it you punctuate each word, staring down the cranky toddler and the feuding siblings in your rearview mirror as you bellow at the top of your lungs, "You'd better stop it! You had *all* better stop it right now or—"

The "or" is cut short by a plastic Happy Meal toy that sails forward from the rear of the van. The still-harnessed thrower squeals with delight as a big-headed, skinny cowboy in a vest ricochets off your head and lands in a small heap on your shoulder.

The last two things you remember are your eyelids twitching in unison and the time blinking green on the van clock:

8:41 A.M.

Signs of an Explosion

I should have seen it coming that morning in the van—and yes, it *is* a true story! If I had had any sense at all (let's not go there!), I would have put a lid on the Big Freeze and just taken my chances with the glass bottle. The checkbook worries, the need for Midol, the twitching eyelids—they were all warning signs, fairly screaming for all to hear (with the exception of the three hearing-impaired children in the rear of my van)…that *she's gonna blow!*

There are warning signs and signals for just about everything that can be potentially dangerous. Train whistles and crossing lights caution motorists to slow down and be observant. Tornado sirens drone loudly as we scurry to a basement or other protective space and scan the skies for a dreaded funnel shape. However, unless you're trained to recognize these warning signs, they are ineffective in helping you remain safe and protected. You have to *know* the warning signs that spell imminent danger—especially when *you're* the one in danger of exploding in anger.

Let's look at three actual warning signs that indicate a volcanic eruption is nearing. Those of us mothers who

experience volcanic anger and explosions can use these
warning signs as a signal to ourselves of an impending
blowup.

Warning Sign #1:
Swarms of Smaller Earthquakes

Did you know that, hours before Mount Saint Helens
erupted on May 18, 1980, *hundreds* of small earthquakes
were recorded in the state of Washington? One after another,
tiny tremors registered on seismic recorders in the area,
clearly indicating activity deep beneath the earth's surface.
One earthquake triggered another until soon the area surrounding the volcano was swarming with seismic activity.
And history books tell us what happened after that. Simply
put, she blew!

Our lives as mothers are filled with all kinds of little
earthquakes that occur in response to the mountain of pressures in our lives. Each one of these pressures, taken by
itself, might not be enough to set off an explosion. All of
them, taken together, bring us to the point where an eruption is imminent. Let's take a look at a few of these trig-
gering pressures and consider how they might influence
our tendency to explode in anger.

Laundry Room Rumbles

If you have kids, you understand the expression *"piles"*
of laundry—unending, unconquerable piles. I'm telling
you, I can have all the laundry done at 10:47 P.M., and when
I return to the utility room at 9:14 A.M....AIEEE!! It's alive!
I'm willing to testify that the towels and underwear have
spawned and reproduced! It's the only way to explain it!

The simple truth about laundry is that it is never done.
This depresses me. More to the point, it annoys me, and I
can't seem to get past the annoyance.

I've tried praying for each child as I fold clothes. I've tried thanking God for the blessings of towels, dishrags, jeans, underwear, and bras...no, I take that back—I am *not* thankful for bras. I've tried, but I always come to the same conclusion: I don't like laundry. And dealing with pile after never-ending pile of laundry just makes me mad.

And what do I *do* when this earthquake is set off? More than likely, I will snap at a child or two and announce that I will no longer do their laundry if it isn't sorted and in the utility room. I may conveniently forget to wash a requested shirt or pair of pants if I had to recover it from underneath a bed. I will probably fold jeans haphazardly and complain when I have to iron them two days later. There is a definite tectonic shift in my attitude and my actions when I have to deal with piles of laundry.

TimeOut/Tamer: If piles of laundry—or any other visual annoyance—tend to shake your temper, find a way to put them out of sight until you can do something about them. For instance, close the door to your laundry room or, if your laundry room doesn't have a door, take a tension rod, throw a sheet or some material over it, and say goodbye to the constant reminder of piles of undone clothes.

Kitchen Quakes

It doesn't matter if you stay home or work outside it for 23 hours a day—a clean kitchen is nigh impossible to keep in a house full of kids. Have you ever walked into this room and just broken down crying over the crusty cereal bowls? That's not even to mention the gunky juice glasses, the crumbs on the counters, the spills on the floor. No matter how much we rinse and stack and scrub, the food messes seem to stay just ahead of us…and with every sticky footstep the pressure builds.

What happens when a mom gazes at dirty dishes and perfectly good food left out overnight? I've been known to throw it quite dramatically to our pet in the backyard and threaten everyone with salmon patties for breakfast!

Technology Tremors

There's nothing more discouraging than finishing up that Human Resources report or a letter to your sister and then watching it disappear in the blink of an eye—as the hard drive crashes or the modem missends or the electricity blinks off and the machine reboots without saving the file you were working on. There's nothing more dismaying than bailing out a clogged toilet or fiddling with a vacuum cleaner that won't vacuum.

Whether they happen in the family room or the workplace, technology woes are always enough to put a mom in a swell frame of mind as she returns to a kitchen full of crusty dishes and a laundry room piled with clothes.

Workplace Woes

Who doesn't feel the magma boiling after attempting to decipher a new supervisor's temperament and modus operandi? I feel earthquake written all over this one! At work you may feel as though your every move, decision, and action is being scrutinized from afar…and the seismic rattles are quick to start. If you work for yourself or as a stay-at-home mom, the pressures may be different, but they're still just as effective at bringing on eruptions. And unfortunately, the stress doesn't end when you leave work. How many times have you blown it with your kids only minutes after stepping in the door?

Seismic Finances

What is there about money that sets off the deep-down rumblings? Declining checkbook balances, mounting credit-card debt, the mailbox full of bills—any of these things are enough to trigger an emotional earthquake. And perhaps *you* have never received a call from a bill collector or a credit bureau, but I have it on good authority that these are especially effective if they come when you have company or your parents are within hearing range. Heaven help the clueless child who approaches you soon after and comments, "I need more stuff."

TimeOut/Tamer: Remember the Old Testament story of Jonah, who enjoyed the shade of a gourd vine, but fell into a snit when the gourd died? God reminded him that, instead of griping, he should be thankful that he had the gourd in the first place. That's a good thing to remember when you find yourself beginning to seethe over hours lost because of something that has gone wrong. Instead of fretting over the problem, try thanking God for the gift of the computer or the washing machine, which has saved you so much trouble in the past. A little perspective and a little gratitude can really help you keep your cool!

Little Triggers, Big Eruptions

The situations mentioned above are not the actual earth-quakes—they are the triggers that set the earthquakes off. And they are far from the *only* possible triggers. (You might have noticed that they are stresses I personally find tend to set off earthquakes in my own life.)

But the more little daily stresses you experience in your life, the more little quakes you'll notice in your life. I'm talking about the rumbles of discontent and annoyance, the tremors of irritation, the clenched teeth and shallow breaths and sharp remarks that signal a shift in your attitude. The more often these tremors occur in the course of your days and weeks...the greater the chance of an actual eruption. When the ground starts shaking even a little, it just makes sense to pay attention.

Warning Sign #2: Sulfur Dioxide Emissions

As a volcano nears eruption it will release toxic gases that can endanger human life and health. If you get too close... watch out!

This was certainly true for me during the more volcanic times of my life. As I struggled with anger toward my children, the warning signs often piled up like leftovers at Thanksgiving dinner, and one of the most obvious was the poisonous tone of my words and comments.

My speech was truly toxic during those early years. Angry retorts sprang easily to my lips, and sarcasm was my specialty. Oh, I was good with those little barbs. They were my habitual response to almost any irritation—until the day I heard them echoed back to me by my son, who was only four at the time.

I can't recall what we were baking, but I had forgotten an item and said aloud to myself, "Oops, I forgot—I needed chips for this!"

Ricky Neal looked at me, rolled his eyes in a manner similar to what he had seen his mother do, and said, "Duuuuh!"

Just one word from his mouth, but it summarized the tone of my speech that year...graceless and unforgiving.

My young children were modeling their speech on their mother's toxic language. (I'll say more about toxic language later.)

But the toxic emissions of those days weren't all verbal. The rolling eyes were part of it as well. So were the exasperated sighs, the furious looks. The emissions from this Mount Momma were a lethal blend of sarcastic speech and body language that reeked negativity. All too often, they culminated in full-scale eruption.

Warning Sign #3: Physical Swelling of the Slope

As a volcano nears eruption, its sides will start puffing out from the pressure inside. There just isn't enough room inside the mountain to contain all the magma brewing and building. It simply doesn't look right—and experts know that funny appearance spells trouble!

I have to admit this warning sign posed a bit of a problem to illustrate. Granted, I could write an entirely different book on physical swelling due to salt intake, but how was I going to paint a picture for you of a human volcano swelling and ready to blow? I was stumped...until I came across a journal entry from 1993. It related an experience I had managed to successfully repress. Trust me, you'd do the same!

TimeOut/Tamer: Never trust a sweet elderly lady. (Just kidding.)

It was late July in 1993. Kristen was almost five years old, and Ricky Neal was three and a half. Rick had been given a transfer to Macomb, Illinois. We were thrilled over the new job, which represented more money and responsibility for Rick. We were also happy with the prospect of moving closer to family. But I was less than enthused over the prospect of shopping once more for the elusive "decent rental" in another small town.

By the way, may I add the following? If you are a landlord, please be advised that "decent" does not include:

- walls painted blueberry blue or rust-orange
- an apartment-size oven unable to handle a large pizza or small turkey drumstick
- two half-hinged metal boxes as "kitchen cabinets"
- red shag carpet as a wall covering

To supply "decent," all you have to do is apply a coat or two of boring beige, keep the walls carpet-free, and look for low-priced cabinets at JR's Used Furniture and More. Who knows? You might save yourself a scenario like the following one.

As it turned out, I had two weeks to find a rental property in a town 97 miles away from our current home. Since Western Illinois University (located in Macomb) also happened to be resuming classes in less than a month, rental properties in town were going quickly. And you have to understand that this was our sixth move in about six years. I was fed up with Clorox boxes, strapping tape, and rental living rooms. The prospect of one more round of house hunting filled my heart with dread. But it had to be done, so I summoned my courage, grabbed my green highlighter, and started scanning the copy of *The Macomb Shopper* that Rick had brought back from his final interview.

I wasn't really picky. All I *needed* was a clean three-bedroom house, located in a safe neighborhood. I would give on a dishwasher (foregoing the extra storage space). I would give on a basement if necessary (foregoing a tornado hideout). I would give on about anything, but *needed* a clean house and a safe neighborhood.

I thought.

After scanning the classifieds I was left with three possibilities.

The first rental property sounded tempting, but the monthly charge was just enough to rule out the possibility of both eating and paying rent.

The second property was more reasonable, but boasted about 900 square feet of living space and the frat boys of IMA GONNA PARTY occupying the dwelling across the street. Pass.

The third rental sounded promising. I even called and spoke with a sweet elderly lady, who assured me that the house was spacious, clean, and in a safe neighborhood. I believe it even had a great room.

I carefully explained that we had two small children and that their being able to play safely outside in a large enclosed yard was very important to us. She assured me that the house was located in an ideal location.

I stressed to her that I would be traveling quite a distance with two little ones and we would need to have immediate possession of the home if we chose to rent. She assured me that it was ready for immediate occupancy.

The following morning I loaded up my two little ones, a container of Oreos, and enough juice, so it seemed, for a houseful of frat boys. I told the children all about our new house and how nice it was going to be because the sweet elderly lady had assured me of it.

We all cheered as we entered the Macomb city limits. I noticed several towering dormitories and mentally crossed off living *anywhere* in the vicinity of a university dormitory or fraternity house. We picked up Rick at his new workplace, and our sweet little family eagerly drove toward our new rental home to meet our new sweet little landlady.

Sigh.

Four gas-station inquiries later, we finally found the street. That's when I began perspiring. But surely this wasn't it! This street wasn't wide enough for two golf carts to pass, let alone two cars. And where was the sidewalk for the children to ride their bikes on? I looked to one side and nearly passed out. Surely that wasn't a university dormitory towering just across the street!

My hands became more and more clammy as we counted down house numbers aloud: 231, 229, 227, 225…*225?* My intestines began to cramp, and I almost threw up.

There it sat—a dirty, weather-beaten ranch-style home with a two-foot-deep front yard and an equal expanse of grass behind the house. Not a fence was in sight. There were no sidewalks, and I had a strong suspicion that the "great" room was going to be anything but.

We stopped and prayed for a miracle.

The Lord did not return.

Rick and I unloaded the kids and made our way to the front door. We knocked and nearly punched a hole through its hollow veneer surface. I turned the knob and discovered that it was unlocked. Hesitantly we stepped into the room and were immediately hit with an aroma of warm garbage and fresh paint.

This would be the great room.

Ricky Neal crinkled up his three-year-old nose and declared, "It stinks!" He then proceeded to gag and produced a dramatic dry heave or two.

Oh, my friends! The magma of frustration was rising and causing some serious deformation of my outer crust! As I angrily muttered, "This is un-be-liev-able!" the sweet elderly lady barreled through the back door into the kitchen. A kitchen in the loosest sense of the word, I might add.

"Hey! Are you going to take it or not?" she introduced herself sweetly—as sweetly as arsenic.

Now, let me preface the following with these facts:

- I was premenstrual
- I was hungry
- I was sick of blue walls and rusty metal kitchen cabinets
- I was already anticipating a second house-hunting trip within the week

And what happened was that I looked Aunt Bee's evil twin in the face and let loose a barrage of verbal lava. "You told me there was a yard!" I stomped dramatically to the living room window, scraped up a layer of crust, and continued, "You told me this house was ready to move into today if necessary!" I felt like hitting something, and the pitch of my voice rose with each word I spit out. "I just drove 97 miles to see this place, and it smells like garbage! There's nowhere for my children to ride a bicycle, and I'd have to wait till Christmas to get an ice cube from that sorry excuse for a freezer!" I ended the litany of injustices with arms folded across my chest and a steely glint in my stare.

At this point Ricky Neal stepped forward, looked the landlady in the eyes, and repeated, "It stinks" (heave, heave, gag, gag).

Rick—volcano expert that he is—saw the warning signals of Mount Momma right before his eyes and ushered the children to the safety of the van. He returned for me—somewhat hesitantly, I might add!

As we were attempting to leave, arsenic-lady spewed a few toxic emissions herself: "I should never have agreed to show the house to you! I should have known you'd be a waste of my time!"

That was it! I lurched forward, ready to body-slam grandma and make myself feel a little better in the process! Instead, Rick forced me to the van as I whispered beneath my breath, "Let me at her."

As Rick closed the door behind me, I caught a glimpse of myself in the van window. My face was a mottled red shade, and it seemed that even the hairs on my head were puffy!

I had experienced the swelling of the slope—and blown it good!

TimeOut/Tamers: Learning to recognize the physical signs of anger can help you gain control over them and stop your anger from escalating. Here are a few physical responses that could indicate the onset of anger.[1] They're sure-fire signals that you need to take action to avoid an eruption!

- feelings of fear, helplessness, frustration, disappointment, being threatened, exhaustion, or panic
- shallow breathing or holding one's breath
- tense muscles
- tight jaws or clenched teeth
- a flushed feeling as your body temperature rises
- a flushed face and a burst of energy caused by a rush of adrenaline

Real Mom Points to Ponder

1. What are some of the physical and emotional signals that usually let you know you're going to blow?

2. In the past, what actions have helped you short-circuit your explosions?

3. Has anything changed in your life recently that makes you more vulnerable to explode these days?

4. Next time you have an explosion or a near explosion— stop and scribble down what happened right before. Ponder how you might prevent a similar explosion in the future.

Underground Issues

Understanding Why She Blows

I am so ashamed of who I am at times. I pray for mercy. God, please withhold your rightful anger from me. I was so angry at Kristen today. Now I am literally sick to my stomach. Where does this fury come from? How on earth can a two-year-old make me so crazy! It's as if I have become someone else. I never thought I would become like this as a mom. Does this come from sin? Is it just me? Is it because of lack of love? Oh, God! Is it possible I don't love my child? I want to be a mother who isn't like this! What a horrible, ugly, mess! God, where does it come from?

I wrote those words in my personal journal on one of my worst days. At the time, I truly wondered whether I really loved my children. After all, what mother who truly loves her child would act like I did? What mother who truly loves her child would wish her away? I desperately needed to believe something—even something as horrible as that I didn't love my children—in order to deal with the enormous weight of guilt and shame I carried upon my heart!

Well, I know better now.

I know it is perfectly possible to love your children and still act like a total maniac. It isn't good. It isn't healthy. But it's possible. And it happens—all the time.

Down Deep

I think we all know—deep within our being—that the rage that flares against our children is usually rooted in something greater than the children themselves. But it is *so* much easier to lay the blame on our children. Blaming them requires less effort than actually examining our lives and considering the real sources for our erupting anger.

Every volcano, after all, has its beginnings deep underground. In fact, the source for every volcanic eruption lies deep beneath the earth's surface in the upper mantle, where the heat and pressure are strong enough to bring rock to the melting point. Mounting pressures eventually push this superheated magma to the surface until it finds a weak spot in the earth's crust and breaks through as a volcano.

The more I've studied, the more I can see that's a pretty good description of what happens in a mother's life to make her "blow." As I've searched within my own life, listened to hurting mothers, and read detailed and sometimes brain-numbing theories of experts, a three-point pattern leading to explosive anger has seemed to emerge.

First, we all have a "mantle" of deep underground issues that includes what we were born with and what has happened to us in the past. These *mantle realities* make up who we are and shape the lens through which we view and deal with life. Much of our anger builds upon them.

Now, many of these realities were determined long before you or I ever thought of becoming a mom, and we have little or no direct control over them. Dealing with mantle realities, therefore, is not so much a matter of changing them, but of discerning their influence and adapting our mothering in light of their existence.

Secondly, building upon this mantle of underground issues are the little and the large stresses of living life in the real world. Family schedules, finances, other relationships, and even our own attitudes exert powerful pressures on us as women, wives, workers, and mothers and can add surprising heat and energy to our underground anger. These pressures can build and build until something comes along to set off an explosion—and our lives can become a walking book title: *She's Gonna Blow!*

This leads us to the third and final point in the pattern. In the lives of most of us that "something" that sets us off is our child or children. In this chapter I refer to them as our precious little trigger points. Because they *are* precious…if we can ever get back to a mental state where we believe that again. And they *are* trigger points—because they seem to have an uncanny knack for finding that weak spot in our crust that lets loose all that built-up heat and pressure.

Sometimes they do it on purpose. Other times they are simply at the wrong place at the wrong time. But because they are there, they're almost always the first ones to get burned by the explosion.

In the following chapters we'll look at each of these three points in greater detail. As you read, I want to challenge you to "think deep." Consider all the potential sources for your anger—both in your past and in your present. When you catch a glimpse of one—or more likely, when one hits you square between the eyes—you can determine then and there how you can successfully accept, adapt, or change your mothering.

Violent eruptions of Mount Momma *are not* inevitable. There's no way to avoid some heat and pressure in your life, but there are ways to avoid a dangerous buildup and an explosive result. Before you can prevent the problem, though, you have to know what's there. So let's do a little exploring.

Pressures from the Past

A number of years ago I received a phone call that pulled the rug out from under my life. It came from my birth father, a man with whom I had never spoken, whom I could not even recall visually from my pre-adoption years. "Julie Ann, this is your father in Texas," he began.

Hmm, I thought. *My father lives in Missouri—who does this guy think he is?* Trust me, having your birth father call you out of nowhere can *really* stir up the underground issues in your life!

I have a hard time recalling our entire conversation. But I do recall his telling me that he loved to write and was in fact hoping to have a book published.

Well, that was music to the ears of an adopted child! At last I could identify my passion for the written word with someone—and not just someone, but my honest-to-gosh birth father. Imagine—my father and I sharing a common bond and "family" trait. I caught myself letting go of the emotional ambivalence I was harboring towards him and began to allow myself to enjoy his unexpected entrance in my life.

I insisted that he send me a copy of the book. He promised that he would, and then our once-stilted conversation turned to his reminiscing about my babyhood and telling me about my five brothers and sisters. Tears rolled down my face as I, an adopted only child, heard tales of protective older brothers holding me close and a sister looking for my face in crowded streets years after my adoption.

We hung up, neither of us ready to commit to further contact. I was content to revel in the newfound sense of connection with my past and with a father who shared a love of writing with his biological daughter.

The book arrived a few days later, and I began to read, eager to see any resemblance to my own writing style. I got about as far as the third chapter. His autobiographical stories gave stark details of his childhood and his own adult family of a wife and six children, including me. He spared no details, and the details were difficult to accept.

Growing up, you see, I had pieced together a rough idea of what my birth family was like. Or better said, I had *imagined* what my birth family was like on the basis of a few snippets of truth. My adoptive grandmother had known my birth family, and when I asked any questions, she had always told me what she knew. According to her, I was the youngest of six children, and our parents had been hopeless alcoholics, chained to either a bottle or a bar stool. Extended family had watched out for us to a certain extent, but my oldest sister, Debbie, and brother, Nelson, had largely been responsible for watching me and my two young sisters and brother.

I knew that we were taken out of the home and put into social service custody as a result of my father's falling asleep in a drunken stupor and catching a mattress on fire. All of us had escaped the burning home without injury, but he and the county had realized the imminent danger we children were in. With little or no counseling, my siblings and I were quickly splintered into various foster care situations, and the county proceeded to terminate all parental rights of both my mother and father.

I don't remember my oldest sister, Debbie, at all. I had been told that she had approached me once on a busy sidewalk when I was window shopping with my adoptive mother. I wish I could remember that. Debbie died in an automobile accident when I was around ten years old.

My oldest brothers, Nelson and Billie Lee, are also a no-show in my pre-adoption memory. It was Nelson who reportedly pushed me off an outside gas tank, which broke my leg. As crazy as it sounds, I wish I could remember that, too.

I lived with my two younger sisters for a year or less in the foster home of Bonnie Patrick. We slept in bedrooms decorated with thick bedspreads and giggled together as we pushed one another on a swing set just beside a vegetable garden. Then one day a couple came to the house and promised Colleen and Lori hamburgers and a ride through town. I stood behind Aunt Bonnie, as all her foster children called her, and watched as my four- and five-year-old sisters were driven out of my life.

I wish I didn't remember that.

Yet all the sense of loss I felt from these things I had been told and longed to remember or forget was nothing compared to the sheer loss of being I felt as I read my father's writings. In one fell swoop, that manuscript obliterated what few ideals I possessed about my birth family and wiped out the childhood fantasy of "happily ever after" that had sustained me for more than 24 years.

We hadn't all gone on to live happy, normal lives with adoptive parents. My oldest sister's death was in part because she ran from the reality of an irretrievably broken relationship with the siblings she remembered all too well. My brothers abandoned their adoptive homes and sought solace in alcohol and drugs. One of them, paralyzed from the waist down, had tried to end his life through asphyxiation by gas. He succeeded in blowing up his apartment and suffered third-degree burns over his body.

I continued reading and then, horrified, I noticed that my birth father had used an alias for everyone *except* me. His odd ramblings about Julie and her pretty dark eyes and the olive tone of her skin caused an alarm to sound deep within me. When he began comparing his memory of me to a girlfriend he had found sexually attractive in his past, I put the book down and absolutely lost it emotionally. I could not believe my birth father had committed such words to paper—words that read like an incestuous ode to his youngest daughter!

That morning I wept for the painful reality of the family that gave me birth. I wept for the loss of unrealistic—but treasured—dreams of what might have been. I wept for the 27-year-old wife and mother who now knew more than she ever wanted to know—and wished she could forget. I wept for everything that was irreparably lost and now shattered beyond repair.

That phone call from my father set off a chain of events that ended up in my seeking counseling for questions and fears long suppressed. I was angry, disappointed, disgusted, afraid, and worried. I wanted answers to the questions that persisted in spite of adult rationality and reason. Above all, I wanted peace with my past.

How could two adults love alcohol more than they loved their own children? Why couldn't I have shared a normal relationship with five brothers and sisters? Why didn't aunts, uncles, and other relatives take us in and keep us together as a family?

I had always believed—wanted to believe—that I had come out of the entire adoption process unscathed and unharmed. I had always believed that I alone, out of six children, had not suffered any form of abuse. But now I wasn't so sure.

I had never allowed myself to think too deeply about this particular belief until that day with my father's manuscript. Suddenly, I was forced to consider scenarios I had never imagined and had to reconcile myself to the fact that I would never know all the details of my past. Sooner or later, with or without that phone call from my past, I would have had to deal with the emotional consequences and fallout of alcohol's grip on my birth family, of my subsequent adoption, of the realities of a family torn apart. I would have had to face the reality that the way I treat my children today has a strong connection to what happened to me in the past.

Pressures Handed Down

To a greater or lesser extent, that's true for you as well. Chances are, your anger toward your children has its deepest roots in underground issues from your past. Any traumas you experienced in your early years—a divorce, a sibling's illness or death, or just painful misunderstandings—are sure to play a significant role in your own family further down the road of life. And if you were abused, the stakes get even higher.

I found the following statement in the midst of a rather long but highly recommended study on abuse put out by the Heritage Foundation: "John Bowlby of London's Tavistock Institute, one of the world's leading experts on the mother-infant relationship, concluded in a 1986 article that the absence of an early infant attachment between mother and daughter increases the likelihood that the daughter, as an adult, will abuse her own children."[1]

Mr. Bowlby's observations struck a sensitive chord deep within my soul. You see, I was three years old when I was adopted. I had been in foster care for a year before that, and two years before, when I was born, my mother was already far gone into her alcoholic state. I've often wondered if she ever held me much, or fed me, or sang lullabies to me as I fell asleep against her breast.

Then just last year, I contacted the caseworker who had been in charge of my adoption. She was more than 80 years old, so I wasn't expecting too many details. She remembered my adopted grandmother and was able to name the judges, lawyers, and county jurisdictions involved in the legal process. However, when I asked her more personal questions, such as who had cared for me in those early years or how many foster homes I had been placed in before adoption, she became quiet.

Uncomfortable with her silence, I prodded her, asking whether she had kept any paperwork from that time or maybe a personal journal that could help jog her memory. She was silent for a long minute and then quickly said, "Oh, I didn't keep any records...I didn't want to remember anything about my cases."

So I was left knowing that in all likelihood I didn't form any attachments with my birth mother or any substitute mother in those early years. And as hard as it is for me to fathom, I may have experienced other kinds of abuse as well. Statistically, I had and still have a greater risk of abusing my children than a child whose early life was nurturing and sheltering.

For those of us who suffered any form of physical, sexual, or emotional abuse as children, the prospect of raising our own children can be daunting. How do we know we won't hurt our beloved little ones? How do we overcome the learned instincts that came as a result of our own pain and go on to deal with our children in a godly and peaceful manner?

The truth is that odds really *are* against us. Child abuse is an injury that tends to repeat itself—despite sincere vows and promises of changing. But my own experience and the experience of many others affirm that we can beat the odds. We *can* choose to raise our children in an abuse-free and nurturing environment, but only if we take steps to deal with the painful underground issues of our own past. We need to acknowledge what happened to us—especially the deep anger that may still be boiling within. We need to work toward forgiveness of those who abused us—for only through forgiveness will we be truly set free. And we need to learn new parenting skills to replace those that were taught to us by faulty teachers.

But we've got to realize that we can't simply *think* our way into positive and changed behavior. We can't simply realize what's wrong and then decide to change—the patterns of early upbringing are just too strong for that. Quite simply, we can't do it alone—but we don't *have* to do it alone!

In my own life, I have found that kind of true, lasting, change only through the power of Jesus Christ. A legitimate, godly counseling service can help. Such help is available through both public and private sectors. You will find a listing of possible sources in Appendix B. I urge you to use them and to seek help for yourself and your children.

TimeOut/Tamer: If you were raised to believe that feeling angry is wrong, you may have trouble even *knowing* that you're angry. The trouble is, suppressed anger doesn't just go away—it tends to show itself in a variety of sneaky, destructive ways. Any of the following ongoing symptoms might be a clue that you have some anger issues:

- a taste for very sarcastic or biting humor
- overcheerfulness
- procrastination
- boredom
- depression
- chronically stiff neck or shoulder muscles

Real Mom Points to Ponder

1. What experiences from your past might be an issue for you when it comes to anger in parenting?

2. Have you ever sworn not to do something to your children that was done to you—and then found yourself doing just that?

3. What positive skills from your childhood do you find yourself repeating?

4. Who would be your ideal role model as a parent? Why?

Pressures from Within

Another important underground issue that affects our behavior consists basically in who we are—our physical makeup, our temperament, and our thought processes.

For instance, some of us are by nature more volatile and likely to "blow" than others. Some of us are more sensitive to the petty annoyances of life, and emotions such as anger rise more quickly to the surface. Some need more sleep than others and react badly to fatigue. A tendency toward depression or anxiety or a predisposition to develop migraines or other painful, temper-shortening conditions can be part of our genetic makeup. So can a tendency toward alcoholism or other addictions. (Because of my family history, I have long known that drugs and alcohol are substances I don't dare become involved with.)

Science has yet to draw a definitive line between characteristics that are learned and those that are inherited. However, as an adopted child, I can affirm that there are many traits in me that have nothing to do with the way I was raised by my adoptive parents. Furthermore, as a mother I am absolutely convinced that my children emerged from the womb with distinct (and *strong*) personalities that affect the way they feel and handle stress.

I absolutely believe that some of the ways we react to the circumstances of our lives—even the way we tend to erupt in anger—are simply built into the basic reality of who we are. They are part of the individual way the Creator shaped us through our genetic inheritance from our biological mother and father.

This does *not* mean that we are "programmed" or "destined" to be angry and abusive. But it does make sense to consider this mantle reality as we try to cut down on the number of Mount Momma eruptions in our lives. The more we can understand ourselves and make adjustments in the areas of our weakness, the more effective we will be as mothers.

This is certainly true of the basic biological fact of being a woman. Being female means a number of positive things—the ability to bear children (yes, it is a blessing!), a higher tolerance for pain, possibly a better integrated brain. Unfortunately, it also means being subject to hormonal shifts that can make most of us a little bit crazy some of the time—and a few of us truly explosive.

I just turned 35, for instance, and these days I'm a wreck! My period has begun showing up sporadically, which often sends me scurrying to the "feminine needs" section at the store for home pregnancy testers. I've finally started buying the two-pack because I know that within the next six months I will probably have good cause to suspect a pregnancy.

I have a college friend who is also 35. She was just told by her family doctor that she is in early, *early*, menopause. As you'd expect, she is less than thrilled with this diagnosis, but at least she can tag her previously unexplainable crying jags on something other than her husband's behavior!

PMS, pregnancy, menopause—any of these natural experiences in a woman's life that involve hormonal changes also have the ability to affect the way she responds to her children. Once again, they're not excuses for bad behavior, but they *are* important influences to keep in mind.

TimeOut/Tamer: You can do your children a favor and help them learn about human behavior by explaining to them that sometimes you're more likely to blow than others. Mark your PMS or high-stress times and warn your family. You could even draw a "Ther-Momma-ter" to indicate your propensity for "blowing it" on a given day. Teach the kids that when the red mercury starts rising, Momma is more apt to blow it…so they should behave accordingly!

Real Mom Points to Ponder

1. What physical conditions tend to make you more susceptible to anger, irritation, or shifting moods? (Think about headaches, allergies, aching feet, insomnia—whatever tends to shorten your temper.) What can you do to keep these pressures down?

2. Do you have any anger about the way God made you?
   Can you honestly say "thank you" to God for your
   mental, emotional, and physical makeup? Why or why
   not?

Mounting Pressures: Cheerios Between Your Toes

Not too long ago I found myself about to go downstairs in
the middle of the night to fetch a glass of water for a "firsty"
child. I usually leave on some type of night-light, but this
evening I had forgotten, and the whole downstairs was as
dark as pitch. But being the "good" mother that I am, I had
counted off the exact number of steps to the kitchen sink—
27. Take 14 steps down the stairs to the foyer, turn left, and
take 13 more mother-steps to the faucet. Not a problem.

I had made it to about step 19 when I began to notice an
odd sensation. The 1927-issue pine flooring creaked
beneath me as I took steps 20 and 21, experiencing with
each step an increasing annoyance that demanded my
attention. Maybe an old nail had come loose from the
planking and was now piercing my foot. True, it should
have hurt more—but it was 2:45 in the morning and I was
a little dazed.

I gently tugged on the piece of twine that clicks on the
40-watt light bulb over my head. Sitting down, I drew my
right foot to my lap—and heard a light plinking sound.
Hmm. Odd-sounding nail. I bent forward and saw something protruding from between my toes. Oh, no! It looked
like more than one nail was involved!

I bent down…what on earth could it be?

Cheerios? Cheerios! Upon close examination I discovered seven toasty little cereal circles tucked snugly between
my ten toes.

Cheerios. A fact of life for a mother of three children—and an amazingly annoying object to find between one's toes at 2:45 in the morning!

Let's look at a few "Cheerios" details that pressure us during the ordinary routine of life. These things can cause annoyance and frustration and can contribute to our feeling "stuck" as a mom. As a result, we are more prone to blowing it with our kids when they come along and push our buttons.

TimeOut/Tamer: An easy cure for Cheerios between the toes: Wear house slippers!

The Family Schedule

Is it just me, or are we jamming our day planners with far too many things? Most moms I know seem to be incredibly busy people with an incredibly long list of places to go, things to do, and people to see. I know I'm not the only mother who has felt wiped out after a day spent running kids to school, doing errands, going to meetings, and providing further transportation to various afterschool activities! The kids are usually wiped out, too!

The following is a direct quote from a young mother wanting parenting advice from other moms at an Attachment Parenting message board.

> The spring activity calendar has arrived! My son is now 3 and can do all the cool 3-and-up stuff in the Parks and Recreation booklet. I've signed him up for swimming 2 times a week and tumbling 1 time a week, 6 weeks each, and the schedules overlap for about 3 weeks. First question: How much is too much for a three-year-old? We'd do

tumbling on Monday nights, Polliwogs swim
class Tuesday and Thursday, plus story hour at
the library every Thursday and one Tuesday
night a month. Would it be overkill to enroll him
in more things?

Goodness! If I were a Polliwog I'd be too pooped to peep,
let alone swim.

A recent Lou Harris survey asserts that "time may have
become the most precious commodity in the land,"[2] and I
would have to agree. Here I sit typing at a computer, cutting and pasting with technology that does it in the blink
of an eye, and I'm still pushing my deadline! My children
wanted to go to the annual Bushnell Fall Festival kickoff
parade, and I said no. Why? Because I didn't have the
time! My day was packed with shopping for back-to-
school items, making "urgent" phone calls, composing e-mail
messages, and trying to complete an ongoing renovation
of our upstairs bathroom. Whew! I'm tired, and it's only
6:59 P.M. I haven't even considered dinner, paid the Mas-
terCard bill (which my husband probably found out
when he attempted to purchase Chinese take-out today!),
or come up with the menu ideas for the food I *volunteered*
to make for an annual Labor Day party at my sister-in-
law's!

I am definitely dealing with more than my share of
schedule-related stress. Once again I have allowed "things
to do, places to go, and people to see" to accumulate in my
life. Once again I have been caught in a web of busyness
that places unnecessary pressure upon my husband, my
kids, and myself. And once again, I am going to have to
carve out some time—quality time—for myself and for my
family. If I don't, chances are good that we'll all feel the
rumblings from Mount Momma in the days ahead.

Time**Out/Tamer:** Consider limiting your family to two meals eaten in a moving vehicle per week.

Finances

This will be the shortest section in the book. Everything I know about successful budgeting could be summed up in three words.

I know nothing.

Larry Burkett, Ron Blue, and Mary Hunt have nothing to fear from Julie Ann Barnhill's taking over as financial guru to the clueless masses. However, I do know about headaches, sleepless nights, anxiety, Pepsid AC check balances, and the consequences of financial stress in anger, rage, and big-time discontent!

A close friend from college once told me that before she was married, she and her father were sitting on the porch swing discussing her college education, money, and life. Audrey (all of 18 at the time) commented, "Dad, money just isn't that important to me. As long as I'm happy and doing something I love, money just doesn't matter."

Audrey's father, a wise man who knew the meaning of hard work and shoestring budgets, looked her squarely in the eye and stated, "Money isn't important as long as you have it. When all of sudden you don't have it—then it becomes *very* important."

That has certainly turned out to be true for me. Money was never that important to me as a child or a teen. I grew up as an "only," and though my parents were not wealthy, it never crossed my mind that I would really lack for anything. I can remember one Christmas when I couldn't think of anything I really wanted. I had everything an 11-year-old could want that year. (Don't hate me; the story takes a decidedly different and permanent turn in the near future!)

My closets were almost always filled with fashionable clothes, and I was able to do things that my mother had never dreamed of at my age. During one summer in my high school years, I traveled to Europe as a teen ambassador with the organization People to People. I walked along the Aegean Sea, kissed an Italian on the world's largest Ferris wheel, and heard Phil Collins' new release "In the Air Tonight" while driving on a Hansel-and-Gretel-style Austrian mountainside.

Yes, I was expected to work summers, and in our small farming community, this rite of passage was accomplished in a bean field. My first *real* job was "hoeing beans" at age 13 with a crew of five other mature workers. I was going to be raking in $3.25 an hour—and note the "was," because hoeing beans turned out to be the one and only job I've ever been fired from. It seems I missed 90 cotton weeds in one row, an accomplishment that Steve, the foreman, didn't look too kindly upon. I was devastated—*wink, wink*—and I think it was about this time that I vowed to never marry a farmer or live anywhere near soybeans!

The most difficult part was explaining to my dad why I didn't need to be at Moser's Coffee Shop at six the next morning for crew pickup. And he turned out to be a bit more devastated about my loss of income than I was—and I found myself washing dishes at Moser's just a few days later. Oh well, it beat hoeing beans!

In spite of summer jobs throughout high school and college, I think it would be safe to say that I didn't have a clue about money and the pressures its mismanagement could put on one's life. However, I was destined for a major learning experience very soon after the fifth day of a certain December.

On that date, after 21 years of life (18 of them spent with Mom and Dad), I walked down an aisle festooned with English ivy and flickering candles, an unbelievably handsome groom awaiting my arrival. We vowed before God and those present to love each other through sickness and health, for richer or poorer, in good times and bad.

What *I* really meant was *some* sickness but mostly health. For better and *scant* amounts of worse, and *definitely* for richer. Period. No poor anything! Just richer.

It was not to be. My dad asked me to return the Visa card that had carried me along through college, and though Rick and I were lucky enough to get a card of our own—those of you with lousy credit ratings know I'm being facetious!— for some reason the balance just seemed to grow and grow, instead of being paid each month as my mom had done over the years.

Then we found ourselves living on one income and raising children *much* sooner than we had anticipated—or budgeted for. All dreams of traveling to Cancún for a belated honeymoon or purchasing a new this or that were slowly relegated to the "not gonna happen" pile of life. In their place came thoughts about bills—and escalating anxiety.

We were able to muddle along for about four years. By then we had two children, some pretty significant credit card debt, a mountain of medical expenses, and a lot of stress. There is no denying the negative impact that poor financial planning and spending had upon my struggle with anger. As many of you reading this know, having a lack of money to purchase basic necessities for your children is one of the most guilt-producing and stress-inducing aspects of parenting! I remember my parents buying a beautiful snowsuit for Kristen when she was just learning to walk. It was pink and pretty and featured faux fur around the hood and cuffs. It also cost $60, and had they not bought it, my precious daughter would have gone without.

I hugged my parents and thanked them, but deep inside I was cringing. *I* wanted to buy the things Kristen needed. I didn't want to ask my parents for basic things like coats. I felt guilty and miserable as Kristen stayed snuggly and warm in her suit.

Motherhood and marriage had brought dramatic changes into my life, and lack of money was by far the most powerful pressure I felt. I tended to have my biggest, ugliest, most dangerous blowups two days before payday, when the checkbook balance stood at negative $1.12, or two days *after* payday, when the bills had been paid and we had $53.38 for the remaining two weeks.

While the financial tension has eased a bit since those days, I still struggle with the bottom-line issues of money in my life. I still break out into a cold sweat when Rick declares, "We're going to start a budget right now!" I still relax more when there is a good amount of cash in my possession and worry when there is a lack of it. I still struggle with being content with what I have, and I seem to always want just a little bit more—which leads us to mounting pressure number three...

Discontentment and the "Shoulds"

Ten years ago I was invited to the home of a new acquaintance. I had met Stacey at church and thought that we might have a lot in common. She and her husband had eaten dinner at our home, and Stacey and I had agreed that we should get together for "mom" time at her place sometime the next week.

About three days later I called to get directions to her house and was taken aback at the street address. She had named a certain subdivision out by the car dealership. But surely she hadn't meant *that* subdivision. It was in *the* neighborhood! You know what I'm talking about—every town has one. It's *the* neighborhood you tool through with your dissatisfied spouse on negative checkbook weeks just to make yourself feel a little bit more lousy! It's *the* neighborhood that makes you curse your lot in life when you realize you couldn't even afford the lawn tractors being used to cut the yards!

The neighborhood.

Gulp! She lived *there!*

I packed up Ricky Neal and Kristen and headed to Stacey's. If I'm honest—and I am being painfully honest— I was hoping that she lived on a peripheral street of *the* neighborhood. I was hoping she lived in a house that *bordered* the neighborhood but didn't quite make the cut. I wanted her to live in a neighborhood like mine!

Well, she didn't. I pulled up into a concrete driveway— which made me nervous because our car leaked oil—and as she greeted the kids, my eyes were drawn to the gorgeous, professional landscape. That woman had more money in perennials than I had in my checking account! One bag of mulch equaled two cans of baby formula in my neighborhood.

The children followed Stacey inside, and I slithered in behind. As I walked into her living room I heard myself gasp—out loud at that! There before my eyes was a room straight from an Ethan Allen showroom floor. The carpet was plush, the color of a white sand beach. Stylishly swagged across her windows were not cotton panels from the local K-Mart but plush, beautiful, cranberry-red draperies.

Stacey led us all through that stunning room, casually chatting with the children. I was beginning to feel sick to my stomach.

With a faux smile plastered on my green face, I followed Stacey through her well-designed home. The refrigerator was the size of a small toolshed. The snack bar chairs were upholstered in white leather. An enormous television screen filled a family room wall. Finally, we made our way to the basement—which looked a little like my *living room*—and I think it was at that point that I officially passed out.

You know what, moms? I can't remember *anything* about that day other than the twisting knife of jealousy and envy that was gutting my enjoyment. Stacey was a wonderful hostess; she made my children feel welcome, and I'm sure she was a clever conversationalist.

However, I simply didn't hear a word she said. My covetous mind was mulling over the expensive porcelain collectibles ensconced in a cherry curio cabinet. I couldn't get the image of her five-piece matching bedroom suite out of my mind. And I couldn't get over the fact that she and her husband had come to our house...the house that I had been so proud of four days ago and now wished away, along with my limp curtains, non-icemaking refrigerator, and dumpy, inherited furniture!

After an hour or so I had to leave, and Stacey suggested that we get together again. But we never did—and you and I both know why. I had allowed my petty jealousy to short-circuit the building of a friendship.

As a woman, a Christian, and a mother, gaining a sense of contentment has been one of my greatest challenges. And what does that have to do with my anger toward my children? Simply that, for me, a feeling of discontent is almost always a first step toward a full-blown eruption. Whenever I start thinking that I am not good enough, that someone has it better than I do, that my children don't measure up, that my life just hasn't turned out the way I wanted...it won't be long before the sparks begin to fly.

It's so important to recognize that the way we feel and the way we act are very closely related to what we think, what we believe, and what we expect—and a lot of the anger we end up aiming at our children often grows out of faulty beliefs and expectations about the way life is supposed to be. One writer points out three expectations that almost always lead to anger:

- The world *should* treat me better.
- I *shouldn't* make mistakes.
- Other people *should* behave the way I want them to.[3]

Do any of these "shoulds" sound familiar to you? They do to me—because every one of them has been a source of mounting pressure for me at one time or another.

The jealousy and discontent that hit me so hard at Stacey's house clearly had to do with so many of the "shoulds" in my mind—that I *should* be able to own a house as beautiful as hers, that Rick *should* make more money, that I *should* be a better manager of our resources—in other words, that the world should treat me better, that my husband should behave the way I want him to (at the moment), and that I shouldn't make mistakes! And how many other times have I gotten my nose out of joint with my children because "they should know better"?

Our attitudes and beliefs really do make a crucial difference in the way we feel and act. Whenever we find ourselves ready to erupt at our children, it's always good to ask ourselves, "What do I really expect?"—and "Does what I expect have anything at all to do with what is true?"

The Problem of Inappropriate Guilt

Here's another important source of mounting stress that is based on attitudes and expectations, but it has more to do with what we expect of ourselves (and what the world expects of us). This is the nagging issue of mothering guilt. And this one's a real pressure cooker for most of us because we have bought into the assumption that, whatever happens to our children, "it's my fault because I'm the mom." We have let too many voices and too many experts overload us with impossible standards of "good" motherhood—and fool us into thinking that we are personally and completely responsible for every problem in our children's lives.

Think about it. Is your precious son or daughter struggling in some fashion? Are you finding it hard to get to sleep, wondering why she isn't sitting up...or toilet trained...or reading...or being asked to parties...or making the best grades...or doing the "right" thing at the "right" age? Do anxious thoughts torment you as you observe your children's inability to master their "nine-times" multiplication facts or throw a baseball with any proficiency? Do health concerns and your children's susceptibility to upper-respiratory problems plague the winter and spring seasons of your home?

And do you find yourself assuming that, at some level or another, it's *your fault*? Maybe you ate the wrong things during pregnancy...or chose the wrong method of childbirth...or breastfed too long (or didn't breastfeed)...or didn't play the right kind of music for the baby...or supported the wrong method of reading instruction...or were too strict...or too lenient...or, worst of all, struggled with anger toward your children!

Whatever you did, you've probably assumed that you're the one responsible for whatever went wrong. You've probably read a lot of books and magazine articles and talked to a lot of people (including your mom, perhaps) who assumed the same thing!

Who among us mothers hasn't recited the first stanza of the poem penned by Elizabeth Barrett Browning's guilty mother, "How did I mess thee up? Let me count the ways." How we agonize over our failure to be perfect mothers! And that's bad enough in itself because guilt is a heavy burden for anybody to carry around. But guilt is even worse when it adds to our mounting stress and makes us *more likely* to blow up at our children.

Please don't misunderstand me here, though. I'm not saying we shouldn't pay any attention to experts who give advice on how to parent. I'm not saying that what we do as mothers doesn't influence our children. I'm certainly not saying we shouldn't take responsibility for our mothering mistakes.

But listening to advice is *not* the same thing as assuming you're a failure if you don't follow all the advice to the letter—or if your children act in ways contrary to what the experts predict.

Knowing your importance as a mother is *not* the same thing as assuming you're the *only* influence on a child's life. (Isn't it a little arrogant to assume that everything depends on you?)

And taking responsibility for our mistakes is *not* the same thing as wallowing in guilt over our failures or our perceived failures.

There's a purpose and place for guilt in everyone's life. Guilt is supposed to motivate us to make amends for our failures and also to point us toward God's mercy and forgiveness. But it's supposed to be a temporary motivator that points us toward confession and repentance, not an ongoing source of stress in our lives.

When we let ourselves be hooked by the pressure to do everything right and be a perfect mother, all we're really doing is making a Mount Momma eruption more likely.

TimeOut/Tamer: In so many stressful parenting situations, laughter can save you. Take advantage of the fact that children really *are* funny…and let the tension escape through a laugh instead of a tantrum. Try to get in the habit of choosing laughter more often—not critical, sarcastic laughter or derisive "I'm laughing at you" laughter, but healthy, cleansing, "isn't this ridiculous?" laughter. Cultivate this quality and teach it to your children. Read the funny papers together. Share silly jokes. Try to look for the funny side of your everyday dilemmas.

Anger at People Who Are Not Your Kids

Have you ever yelled at your kids (or worse) when what you really wanted to do was wring the neck of your husband…or your boss…or your mother? If you're like me, the real target of your wrath may never have had a clue—but your children did!

I'm smiling as I type this because just two weeks ago I was reading to my husband some of the feedback I had received from my editor. She had thought it a good idea to deal with this very issue of misdirected anger. I agreed, and Rick just stared at me with that "animal caught in the headlights" look.

He said, "Well, you've never had any issues with me that you've taken out on the kids…have you?"

Hello! I reminded him of the issue of my birthday. Seems the man has difficulty remembering July 21, 1965. Things got kind of nasty around our house the last time he forgot—which happened to be three weeks before he asked me that silly question!

TimeOut/Tamer: Never underestimate the power of a sincere apology. When you realize you've misdirected anger toward your children that really belonged somewhere else, admit it. Explain what you've done and say you're sorry. Then take steps to handle your anger, first by confessing it to the Lord and then by taking whatever steps you feel God is leading you to make—working off the angry energy physically, speaking to the person in question, choosing to forgive and let it go...or all three.

Yes—we do let our anger toward our husbands and others get misdirected toward our children, who happen to be handy and rather defenseless targets. This happens even in relatively happy marriages like mine. For those of you who are single moms, perhaps longing for a husband or relationship, or are divorced, struggling to keep everything afloat while dealing with an ex-husband—well, I know from the stories of friends in similar circumstances that misdirecting toward your kids the anger you're experiencing is a reality for you too! The same applies to those taking care of elderly relatives, struggling with unhappy work situations, or working on a church committee with a person who pushes your buttons.

Sometimes we're well aware of who we're mad at and why, but there are reasons we think we can't express that anger toward its real target. Other times we don't have a clue what or who we're really mad at—we're just mad. But the longer we go along with unresolved anger toward anyone, the more likely we are to unfairly unleash that anger on the nearest target...our children.

Real Mom Points to Ponder

1. What Cheerios have been stuck between your toes recently? What is the mounting pressure that most often besets you?

2. Contact a close friend, spouse, or counselor, share with him or her your struggle in this area, and ask for prayer. But be prepared...you may have to explain the Cheerio concept once or twice.

Your Precious Little (or Big!) Trigger Points

Ah yes...children. Parenting wouldn't be the same without them. They *are* precious, but doggone if it isn't hard to see that sometimes in the midst of underground issues and mounting pressures! In fact, I have come to believe that in most cases the immediate cause of angry explosions is...well, a child.

Yes, you read correctly, and I figured it out without a Ph.D. or anything! Most children seem to be born with the uncanny ability to push every button and set off every lava bomb known to motherkind.

Yes, the underground stresses are real.

Yes, Mount Momma eruptions are often about issues not directly related to the mothering role.

But there is nothing like a child to give that final little shock that sets the cinders to flying and the lava to pouring.

What is it about our children that sets us off so easily? I can think of a million answers, but to me they seem to fall into three general categories: the things they do, the things they say and the way they are.

The Things They Do

It was February 1996, and western Illinois was in the middle of a severe winter storm. Six inches of snow had fallen in just a few hours' time, and the wind was piling up impassable drifts on all the highways surrounding our little town. Fierce gales had knocked out our electrical service, and Rick and I found ourselves housebound with a one-year-old baby on an apnea monitor and two antsy older kids who were six and seven years old.

We weren't *un*accustomed to losing power in Prairie City, and so we had several oil lamps burning throughout the house. Nevertheless, our 70-year-old home was still a bit shadowy, and the stairway and front foyer were difficult to navigate. We had gathered in the family room and played as many quiet games as Rick and I could remember, but after another few hours we were quickly losing control.

"Do not run through the house!" I barked as Kristen tagged her brother and took off for the upstairs. "It's dark, and if you get hurt we can't get you to the hospital." (As the mother of boys, I am always aware of road conditions to the nearest hospital!) I didn't hear any screams or running feet, so I assumed all was well.

I sat down at our kitchen table and began reading a book by lamplight. The wind rattled the panes of my kitchen windows, but inside 540 East Main all was safe and sound. Or so I thought until I heard Kristen shout shrilly from somewhere in the dark house. "Moooooooooooom!" she called, "Ricky hit his eye on the corner of the column."

"Was he running?" As if I had to ask!

"Yeah…but I think he's really hurt—you'd better come here, Mom!" (As the firstborn child, Kristen has often taken it upon herself to parent her mother and let me know what I'd better do.)

"Hey, I *told* you guys to knock it off," and I returned—without guilt—to chapter four of a Frank Peretti thriller. About this time Ricky Neal walked into the kitchen with his left hand covering his left eye.

"Now, what did I just tell you? Let me see…" I took a deep breath, still staring at my book and began. "A—I said 'Do not run through the house.' B—I said that if you do get hurt, it's too nasty to go to the doctor or hospital. C—I told you, 'Do not run through the house'!" Then I added a gentle phrase of reproof that many of us have uttered: "*I don't feel sorry for you.* This stuff always happens when you don't lis—" I stopped my diatribe long enough to gaze up at Ricky Neal, and he quickly capitalized on the opening.

"Mom, just look at my eye!" He removed his hand long enough for me to see his eyebrow split wide open, bleeding profusely. I could tell he wanted to cry but couldn't decide if it was safe to or not.

Now, you'd think that seeing my son bleed would have softened my spirit a bit. But no, it just made me see red! (After all, by this point I had seen a fair amount of blood on my son!)

"Ricky Neal Barnhill, how on earth am I supposed to fix that? I told you not to…"

Well, you've gotten the point by now! If Ricky's dad had not come in and saved the day, I'd probably still be going on and on about not running in the house. *I* was *ticked* that he had ignored my wise instruction and run through the dark living room! *I* was *mad* that he had tripped and somehow found the only sharp corner in the entire downstairs area. I was *furious* that we would have one more emergency-room bill for an injury that could have been prevented!

It wasn't until Rick had driven away with my precious son into absolutely insane highway conditions that my heart began to soften. It had taken me more than 45 minutes to consider my child's need rather than what my child had done.

Has anything like this ever happened to you—at a time when the very fact that kids *act* like kids makes you see red?

Somewhere, deep within the recesses of our minds, we know they can't help it. In the deepest part of our mother brain, we know that "kids will be kids," that it's normal and even healthy for them to make mistakes and act immature and even get themselves into trouble. Yet, those moments when they do just that can trigger such frustration—and lead to volcanic responses from us…the sane, calm, caring adults.

For those of you with young children, let's talk about the things they do when they're little. Can we talk socks and toddlers? Can we talk mental breakdown? *Please* tell me that some of you have experienced the "toe seam from Hades" routine? Why are some toddlers' feet so sensitive to such a miniscule seam? These are the same kids that will play barefoot in a sandbox and squish bugs with their naked big toe! Little else brought the magma of my anger to a quicker boil than watching my 35-pound eldest wrestling with a cotton sock and screeching, "Me do! Me do!" And don't forget:

- Toddlers and leaking sippy cups
- Toddlers and toilets and nonflushable objects
- Toddlers and scheduled naptimes
- Toddlers interacting with *(read: physically assaulting)* other toddlers!

Years after I fought with Kristen over sock seams I read a book by Mary Sheedy Kurcinka titled *Raising Your Spirited Child*. What an enlightening read that was! I learned that some children are highly sensitive to textures and there are actually a lot of kids who throw crazy fits over sock seams!

(It is one of the highly recommended books that I have listed in the back of this book. I've also given information for purchasing seamless socks.)

Thankfully, in our house we've been past the toddler stage for several years now. Lately, in fact (for reasons that may have something to do with parenting an 11-year-old and a 12-year-old), I've been reading a lot about children in early adolescence. This age is commonly called the "tween-ager" stage. It's sort of the phase two of parenting, and I'm finding it's quite different from the early years.

In my experience, the trigger points in those early years of parenting usually involved one of three things—a piece of furniture, a window, or some part of a kid's anatomy. Now my furniture actually goes weeks and months without injury. We haven't had a window broken in ages, and for the first time in six years we did not meet our medical insurance deductible for the year! The old things have passed away, but what has replaced them?

Well, for one thing I'm getting *a lot* more attitude. Tweens *do* attitude quite well, and mine have rattled my mantle on more than one occasion. They've also replaced flagrant physical fouls against one another with teasing and head games—though the basic substance of their sibling warfare (an ongoing trigger) hasn't changed.

As I've mentioned before, I grew up as an only child, so some of this stuff I just don't understand. One evening, after refereeing a particularly grueling day of sibling warfare, I asked my husband—who is one of four children—the following:

"So, you wanted to hurt your brother and sister growing up?"

"Yes." (Remember, I'm the talker in the family.)

"Let me see if I have this right. You wanted to cause pain to your older brother and younger sister?"

"Yes."

"And they wanted to cause you pain also? You *all* did these things *on purpose?*"

"Mm-hmm, what's your point?"

Well, I still don't get it, and I probably have more rules for engagement than Rick *ever* did as a child. But what I do finally get is that our children will *always* do things that get under our skin. I'm 35, and I still get the distinct impression that some things I do when I visit my parents really bug them!

Nevertheless, our job as mothers is to not lose sight of the preciousness of who our children truly *are*—no matter what they do. And that isn't nearly as easy to do as it is to say!

TimeOut/Tamer: Have you ever thought to consciously forgive your children for the things they do to make you angry? Yes, I know you forgive them all the time—that's why they're still alive! But a lot of us still harbor little grudges toward one child or another because he or she is "always" doing something that upsets or bothers us (whether or not they "mean to").

We can lessen the stress and improve our relationships if we *consciously* choose to forgive that child. In your journal or in your prayers, specifically name what bothers you and ask God to help you forgive and put the issue behind you. (You may then find that you need to ask the child's forgiveness for your attitude. That can be a great healer, too.)

The Things They Say

Remember watching your baby and thinking, *I can't wait until she talks?*

You wondered what her tiny voice would sound like. Would she say "Ma-ma" or "Da-da" first? Would she talk before her first cousin?

You waited.

You made cooing sounds that she soon learned to imitate, and then she began the baby babble that held you captive for minutes on end. You waited, watching her roll her tongue and struggle to articulate sounds. And then suddenly one day, as you pulled into the driveway after an afternoon of buying groceries and running errands, you heard from the car seat behind you "Ma-ma."

Well, that was it—she had you hook, line, and sinker. In the mornings she would greet you bouncing merrily upon her mattress, "Ma-ma, Ma-ma."

Two weeks later she ensured her place in the family will with "My Ma-ma! My Ma-ma!" As you drove here and there, melodic sounds wafted forward to you: "Luv-oo, Ma-ma."

What sweet days! What blissful memories!

You're now two years down the road, and this is when the plot takes a nasty turn that involves a stiff pointer finger and the word *Mom*.

"Mom."

Poke to the upper thigh.

"Mom."

Poke to the outer thigh.

"Mom."

And it continues—"Mom," *poke*, "Mom," *poke*—to infinity and beyond!

Chances are you'll go completely insane in just under six minutes, depending on the strength of the poke and the nasal quality of the word *Mom*.

Move ahead six or eight years and it's not just the "Mom" that's usually the problem. It's usually "Mom" accompanied with something else. As I said, a poke. Or even worse, a long string of accusations. Or a smart-aleck remark. (This is especially annoying when you can tell they learned it from you.) Or an argument or debate or complaint. Or words of outright defiance...

"Mom! Make her stop!"

"But you said...!"

"But you promised."

"I don't care."

"You can't make me."

"You're a silly ol' poo-poo head!"

It amazes me how innocent these kinds of phrases can look on paper ("poo-poo head" being the notable exception!). It amazes me still more how a simple phrase—"Quit it!" for instance—can send shock waves through the mantle and trigger waves of irritated magma. It seems that we, as adult women, should be able to overcome this, doesn't it? At this particular stage in my children's vocal development, "Quit it!" comes out about four octaves higher than Whitney Houston ever dreamed of! "Quit it!" squealed through tense, tight, vocal chords puts a lot of pressure on Mount Momma!

There are so many ways our children communicate to us that can trigger potential eruptions, from the first "waaaaa" of infancy through the "whys" of toddlerhood and on into the innocent or defiant "whats" of later childhood and adolescence. The real trick is learning to listen *past* all those annoying communications and hear the real message behind them, which is "Mom, I love you and I need you."

If we could hear that every time, we could reduce a lot of the pressure potential in what our children say!

The Way They Are

From the moment my second child came into being, he has been an intensely high-spirited, self-determined, self-confident, no-holds-barred individual. My morning sickness was twice as bad with Ricky Neal than with Kristen or Patrick. He moved sooner and with more gusto in my womb than either of my other two children. In fact, Ricky Neal and I would play a game when I was seven months pregnant with him. He probably doesn't remember it, but I do—and the funniest thing about it was how badly this seven-months-in-the-womb baby wanted to win.

I would lie back against the armrest of our sofa and gently nudge my full belly. I could count out loud: "One, two, three…" Then *punch!* Ricky Neal would answer with a full-throttle kick to my belly button. I would nudge again; he would kick back. On and on we did this, each trying to outlast the other. Each time that I assumed he must be tired and ready to sleep, he would wait just a bit longer…just until I began to grin in victory. Then he would kick back once more—just hard enough to communicate, "I'm still here—and you're not going to get the last word!"

The transition stage of delivery lasted less than 15 minutes with Ricky Neal, and with only three pushes he was officially in the Real World. Immediately he took a gulp of air and began wailing. I have a picture that Rick took of him just moments after birth. His mouth is wide open, his eyes are tightly shut, and he's telling us all about it!

Now—in hindsight—I know that my son was contemplating world domination as he sat in his high chair a few months later. He was riding a bicycle, without training wheels, at age two. Once, when he careened over a four-foot retaining wall and landed on a concrete sidewalk below, he just batted an eye and wanted me to let him do it again!

Whatever Ricky Neal did, he did with gusto and determination. And by the time he was three years old I was worn out and frazzled to the max! Instead of seeing his voraciousness for life as a positive quality, I saw it as hard to handle and annoying. Instead of honoring the attributes bestowed upon him by a loving and all-knowing Creator and then attempting to steer them in a positive direction, I saw those attributes as mistakes, and I was determined to correct them!

To me, he seemed to come from another planet. And the more I thought about it, the more convinced I became that my job as his mother was to *make* him more cautious, *make* him more obedient, *make* him show repentance. In fact, some of my strongest battles with rage have been based on my wanting to *change* him—to *force* him to:

- Slow down! (He'd speed up.)
- Think ahead! (He rushed headlong.)
- Eat more slowly! (He gobbled.)
- Talk more softly! (You could hear him a mile away.)
- Quit wiggling! (He just couldn't!)

But I couldn't—change him, that is! So I did what most mothers do when they have exhausted their own resources, I handed him over to his father—his heavenly Father, that is. That of course was a good move, except that my attitude in doing it wasn't the best.

I prayed—with a distinct whine that sounded a bit like Adam in the Garden after he got caught. "God, You gave me this child." *Read: All the mistakes are Yours.* "And I just can't do anything with him." *Read: I quit.* "I'm giving it all to You and just want to rest in Your will." *Read: Don't give him back until he's fixed!* To seal the deal I quoted the first part of 2 Corinthians 1:20: "For as many as are the promises of God, in Him they are yes"—and waited for Ricky Neal to morph into a perfect child.

Three months later, as you might guess, the "morphing" had yet to occur—but I had another plan. I was scheduled to attend a stay-at-home moms' conference in Bloomington, Illinois. I had registered for several terrific workshops, but the one I was looking forward to most would be led by author and speaker Donna Partow. She would be speaking on temperaments and how they affect the dynamics within a family.

I saw this as the answer to my prayer. Finally! As I sat down in the busy lecture hall where the workshop was being held, I checked the ink level in my pen and prepared to identify, document, and "fix" all of Ricky Neal's temperamental defects.

The session began with prayer, and we were off! Donna began by describing each of the four temperaments and asked us to identify the type or combination of types that best described our own natural tendencies. She gave humorous examples of each, and I immediately recognized my own "sanguine/choleric" leanings. I enjoyed listening to her describe the strengths of this particular temperament combination: tenacious, spontaneous, outspoken, and willing to help.

Yep, when I decide something needs to be done, it gets done, no matter what. I detest schedules that limit my ability to come and go as I please. I am certainly not afraid to voice my opinion, and I don't mind volunteering for things—that is, if I remember to write them down on my calendar. I decided I really liked being a "sanguine/choleric" person.

Next, Donna instructed us to identify the type or combination of types of each of our children and to note down a few descriptive words about that temperament. I quickly scribbled Kristen's name and wrote down the words that best described my firstborn child: V*ery* detail oriented. Tenderhearted. A "deep" thinker. Easily moved to tears.

I asked a question or two of Donna and quickly came to the conclusion that my daughter possessed a strong melancholy temperament. That assessment must have taken all of three minutes. I knew her so well! And besides, I figured I needed all the time I could get to tackle Ricky Neal—the child who needed to be "fixed."

I wrote down his name and then reviewed the handout Donna had given to each of us. Soon I was writing down characteristics like "headstrong," "short attention span," "argumentative," and "forgetful." Then, turning back to the handout, I began to identify Ricky Neal's *problem.*

Let's see, the handout puts "headstrong" under "choleric." "Short attention span" goes under..."sanguine," and "argumentative" under..."choleric," and "forgetful" under..."sanguine."...Wait a minute!

I looked again at my list of "strengths" and saw: Tenacious. Spontaneous. Outspoken. Willing to help (when I remember!).

I looked again at Ricky Neal's list of "problems": Headstrong. Short attention span. Argumentative. Forgetful.

"Oh" (in a very, very, tiny voice).

Ricky Neal's "problem" was—he was just like me!

The painful truth for me was this: *I* am headstrong and argumentative. *I* possess a very short attention span and forget lots of important things. *I* can be hard to handle and annoying as a wife, friend, daughter, and mother. And yes, I am also tenacious, spontaneous, outspoken, willing to help—and a child of God.

It wasn't 15 seconds after the dawning of that truth that Donna resumed speaking. After sharing a story, she uttered some words that I will never forget: "God did not give you your son so you could 'fix' him or whip him into shape. God gave you your son to make *you* more like Jesus."

Yes, she really said *son!* Clearly she had gotten into my personal journals and decided to take me personally to task during her seminar....

Well, that probably isn't true. But have you ever tried to cover up the sound of your crying—no, make that wailing—in a public place and failed miserably? If you were in that workshop and you overheard some wrenching sobs...well, that was me. God melted my cold, judgmental heart that afternoon. For the first time in the nearly four years of his life, I saw *and accepted* Ricky Neal for who he really was.

God answered my prayer. He fixed Ricky Neal by fixing his mother's heart.

TimeOut/Tamer: Looking your child square in the eye and tenderly holding his face in your hands, say, "I love you just the way you are!" Do it at least twice a week, so that the reality of the message can sink into both your child's heart and your heart.

The people who really push your buttons are often not the people who are so different from you, but those who are remarkably like you. How could I have missed that as a mother? I praise God that He lifted that particular veil of ignorance from my life.

I can tell you straight out that my relationship with Ricky Neal began to change that very moment. At that moment, in that lecture hall, I asked God to give me a heart for the individual person my second-born is. I asked Him to forgive me for not seeing Ricky Neal—or Kristen on many occasions—in the light of His goodness. How arrogant of me to insult the Creator by seeing my children as anything but good in the basic makeup He gave them, even (or especially) when they are like me!

Now, am I saying that my little ones have somehow attained sainthood as children? No way! But I *am* saying that my children and yours were put together with a particular purpose in mind. They were given to us by a Creator who wants to teach us more about Himself—and His chief teaching tool for the next several years is going to be the child you call your son or your daughter.

It doesn't matter whether we're talking about a birth child or an adopted child or a stepchild. It doesn't matter if he or she has lived with you since day one or came into your life later. Your children are yours for a reason and the way *they are* is good.

If you can believe this and be thankful—regardless of the underground issues and the mounting pressures and the trigger points that tend to make you blow—you'll find yourself moving toward a much more meaningful, fulfilling relationship with your child.

And that in itself will cut back on the number of eruptions in your life.

Real Mom Points to Ponder

1. Doctors have noted that children tend to throw temper tantrums for the following reasons:

   - They are angry or frustrated because they can't have something they want.
   - They want to get what they want by themselves.
   - They want attention.
   - They are tired, hungry, or irritable.

Now, is it just me, or can most adult women be described in one or more of these ways on any given day? How can realizing your own need for grace help you extend grace to your own children?

2. Consider the ways in which you confront and engage your child. Are they age-appropriate? Or are you dealing with your ten-year-old in the same way you did when he or she was six?

3. List some of your child's basic characteristics that you dislike or that tend to make you angry. Do you see any of these characteristics in yourself as well? How can you learn to appreciate and to be thankful for these characteristics?

5

Volcanic Damage

Recognizing When You've Gone Too Far

Do you believe me when I say I love my children with all my heart? I have lain awake at night and rehearsed in my mind how I would get them to safety in case of an emergency. I've gotten myself "all riled up," as my grandma used to say, over just the thought of someone's seeking to harm them. I love my children fiercely and would give my life for them. And yet there have been times when I asked, in the loneliness of my soul and with the shroud of painful memories obscuring joy, *Have I gone too far? Have I abused my own child?*

I can't think of any mother on the face of the earth who *wants* to answer yes to that question. I find myself hesitating as I type these words, knowing the permanence of my written and printed confession. Yet I must address this difficult truth, this cancerous reality that gnaws away inside more than a few of our lives as mothers.

I must address this issue because no one ever questioned me or raised this subject in my early years of mothering and anger—and my children suffered the consequences. I must address this issue, for it is only after we've acknowledged our absolute worst behaviors and attitudes that we can fully grasp our Father's absolute grace and best for us as women and as mothers!

How Far Is "Too Far"?

Merriam-Webster defines *abuse* as "improper or excessive use or treatment." Oh boy! Who among us reading (or writing) these pages hasn't used improper or excessive treatment with her kids? Who among us hasn't felt convicted for going a little too far in the desire to discipline or corral a high-spirited child? We're all guilty of this at some time in life.

Abuse has also been defined as "the misuse of parental power." That makes complete sense to me. As the mom and as the adult, I should have command of my emotions and actions. It goes without saying that my children should feel safe in my company and that any actions I take physically, verbally, or spiritually toward them should be reasonable and controlled.

However, that has not always been the case in my life as a mother.

Unlike many mothers, who seemed to commit errors of judgment toward their children rarely, I increasingly found myself acting out in an improper or excessive manner toward my children. I never *intended* to go too far. I never *intended* to misuse my parental authority or strength with my children. Yet I admit there have been times when I have dealt physically, emotionally, or spiritually with them in a way that crossed over into "improper or excessive" treatment. One incident in particular comes to mind.

We were living in Effingham, Illinois at the time, and Rick was working as a Loss Prevention Supervisor with

Wal-Mart. In those days, Rick left for work by 5:30 A.M. and generally spent 10 or 12 hours on his feet. When he was done with work, he wanted nothing more than to return home, hold the children in his lap, and relax in his recliner.

What I wanted more than anything in those days was to *leave* the house.

You see, I was also on my feet nearly nonstop in those days—chasing down a toddler and trying to protect my newborn son from his 18-month-old sister's overzealous attention.

It wasn't that Kristen didn't love her baby brother. In fact, she was enthralled with him—*too* enthralled. His forehead demanded to be kissed…hard. The chubby ears (I never knew until Ricky that ears could be chubby!) of our "Buddha baby"—so we called him—demanded to be poked, and once I caught her pulling him across the carpet by his chubby little ankles.

Kristen was so crazy about Ricky Neal that I sometimes resorted to placing him on the floor and turning the playpen upside down over him in order to keep his sister away. Otherwise she would be crawling up and falling in the playpen or assaulting him in some other crazed toddler fashion.

Ricky Neal was an exceptionally hungry baby, and it seemed I was nursing every 45 minutes. Even after I switched to formula, my days consisted of little but bottle liners, burping, diapers, and protecting the baby from his sister! To top it off, I was attempting—as you may remember—to potty train Kristen. Talk about wanting to leave the house!

Then came the afternoon when the fatigue of new motherhood all but overwhelmed me. I desperately needed a nap while Ricky Neal was sleeping and Kristen was napping. But that was the day, of course, that Kristen absolutely refused to stay *in* her room, *on* her bed, or *away* from her

brother. I was forced to make a pallet for Ricky Neal, cover
him with the "cage," and resort to threatening his sister:

"Stay in your room, Kristen Jean! I do not want you to
get off your bed. I do not want to hear you opening the
door. I do not want you to come out of your room." *(I do not
like green eggs and ham!)* "Do you understand Mommy?"

She nodded affirmatively, snuggled beneath her blankie,
and murmured, "I wuv woo, Mommy," as I gently closed
the door behind me.

I sighed. Maybe this would work out after all.

After checking on Ricky Neal one last time, I headed
gratefully to the couch, snuggled against an armrest, and
drifted into blissful sleep…for approximately 12 minutes.

"Mommy! I can't sleep!"

The announcement came quite loudly, right in my ear. I
forced my eyes open to see Kristen standing beside the
couch, her pixie face about two inches from my nose. While
coming out of her room she had awakened her brother,
who was now screaming and demanding attention. I sat
up and stared at my daughter with bleary eyes. Ricky
wailed inconsolably from his pallet, and now I caught the
distinct aroma of soiled underpants…Kristen's.

That's when I lost it.

I scooped her up harshly beneath her arms and held her
at arm's length. Stalking toward her room, I violently shook
her little frame and began weeping as uncontrollably as my
newborn son. I wanted sleep, I needed sleep…and this 18-
month-old was the only reason I wasn't getting any. I was
sick of soiled panties, sick of being too tired to function,
and sick of being disobeyed by my child.

As I approached Kristen's bed, I stopped abruptly, drew
back my arms, and threw her as hard as I could in the general vicinity of her mattress and sobbed aloud, "Now, stay
on your bed!" And in the next instant her tiny body made

contact with a wall decorated with idyllic pictures of babies and bunnies. I never intended this! The blood drained from her complexion, and she gasped. Her eyes were filled with terror, though she did not utter a sound.

Almost instantly, I tasted the bile of fear and regret. I immediately stepped forward, wanting to right what I had just done.

But Kristen flinched, afraid of her mother's touch. My little daughter cowered and shrank back against the cold bedroom wall as I tried to draw near her.

Oh, dear God! I *never* imagined that I would act in such a way as to cause my own child to fear for her safety! It took the fear-shocked gaze of my daughter's eyes to knock me into reality. Today, more than 12 years later, that memory still shocks me—so much that I almost didn't put it in this book.

Was I guilty of abusing Kristen Jean that day, even though no one saw and she wasn't hurt? I believe the answer is, unequivocally, yes. A thousand things could have happened. Her arm could have easily twisted and been broken; she could have hit her head against the sill beneath her bedroom window; any number of scenarios could have occurred. And even though I thank God they didn't come about, I know the truth in my heart: My actions that day were both improper and excessive. I had misused the parental power given to me by God—physically by throwing my child and emotionally by losing control of my actions. That is abuse.

I identify all too well with this observation of Dr. Peggy McHugh, a professor of pediatrics and director of the Child Protection Team at New York's Bellevue Hospital: "Perhaps the greatest tragedy of severe child abuse is that it is so often unintentional, a momentary event, but it can forever change the course of a life....Probably the darkest truth of all is that you can love your children to death and still hurt them."[1]

And what if Kristen *had* been hurt? What would I have done? Would I have taken her to the hospital? To our family doctor? How would I have explained her injuries? What would I have said to her daddy when he asked, "How did this happen?" Would I have told anyone the truth?

I doubt it. I was ashamed and scared to death at what had happened. I would have made up some story and vowed to never let it happen again. And in a sense, I didn't let it happen again. But though I never did *throw* Kristen another time, I still found myself smacking her too often or, more of the time, verbally wounding her with the power of my words.

A Difficult Topic

I know that abuse is a touchy subject in many Christian circles and in churches. Christians believe—and rightly so—that proper discipline is essential to raising godly and upright children. But sometimes I wonder if we're so desperate to hold on to "spare the rod, spoil the child" that we overlook the cold, hard reality of abusive behavior by Christian parents. I believe it's time for the body of Christ to address the fact that many families aren't "disciplining" their children at all, but rather are punishing them in extreme and excessive ways—ways that inflict guilt and grief upon the children and upon the parents themselves.

I have spent the past year doing research on this subject. I've brought home piles of books from the local library. I've also scoured magazines, editorial columns, and "dot-coms" of all kinds until my fingers were numb and my eyes were glazed. Yet it was difficult—no, make that nearly impossible—to find sources that even gave a nod to the issue of abuse within Christian homes. I found *one* article actually titled "Christian Parents Who Abuse," and that article dealt only with physical abuse, not emotional or spiritual abuse.

But abuse is not an "us versus them" issue. We can't say, "It's just those who do not believe in Jesus Christ who abuse." Or, "It's single moms…or poor families…or step-families."

If we simply open our eyes and ears, we can see that such an attitude is foolish, unreasonable, and flat-out wrong. I've heard too many "Christian" parents say things to their children that made my skin crawl. I've heard too many mothers express dissatisfaction with their children so strongly that I find it hard to believe they haven't acted out toward those children in some way. The sooner we stop denying reality and admit that Christian parents and mothers are capable of committing abusive and regrettable acts toward their children, the sooner we can deal with the volcanic damage of anger, no matter what form it might take.

I realize that many of you may have experienced some form of abuse as children, and I recognize the difficulty of breaking the curse of generational abuse. We tend to parent the way we have been parented, and patterns of abuse are easily passed on, even when we don't want to pass them on. (I will specifically address this situation—and some solutions—a little later.) For now, I want to focus not on the *reasons* we abuse our children, but on the *ways* any of us, regardless of our background, can inflict injury upon our children's hearts and minds through physical, emotional, and spiritual abuse.

TimeOut/Tamers: When you feel yourself getting hot under the collar, try to work out the angry "rush" of energy in a way that harms no one—through physical activity and exercise.

Scrub a floor. Run up and down a stairway until you begin to tire. Do jumping jacks and have your kids join you. (I don't recommend using a NordicTrack. I tried doing that when my kids were smaller, but each time the kids would poke me on a sweaty thigh or get bumped with a moving ski, I would rant and rave even louder!)

Physical Abuse:
Excessive and Out of Control

What exactly is physical abuse? A definition I've found helpful summarizes the great many definitions that I have encountered:

> Physical abuse can be defined as [the infliction of] any type of physical injury by punching, slapping, hitting, beating, kicking, biting, arm twisting, hair pulling, burning, or otherwise harming a child. The parent or caregiver may not have intended to hurt the child, and injury may have resulted from overdiscipline or physical punishment that is inappropriate to the child's age. However, it still is abuse. Any physical act causing harm to a child is abuse whether it was intended [to harm] or not."[2]

I would add to that description out of hard experience. I would say that physical abuse is any form of physical treatment or punishment that 1) causes actual harm not only to the body but also to the mind and spirit of the child and 2) results from parental emotions and attitudes that are inappropriate and out of control.

Many families implement some form of corporal punishment with young children, and many draw on biblical guidance in doing so. The ideal is that this physical action be done gently, lovingly, and by a calm and reasonable adult. The ideal for Christian families in particular is that the properly administered corporal punishment will help train a child in obedience to his parents, to other types of authority, and ultimately to God Himself. When these principles are adhered to, I have no quarrel with it.

Life, however, has a way of crushing ideals and replacing them with cold, hard, reality—and mine came in a nine-pound, eight-ounce package labeled Child Number Two.

From the very get-go my high-spirited second-born child, Ricky Neal, was a strong-willed baby. As he grew, well-meaning relatives often counseled me to "rein him in while he's young." Some of the tried-and-true appliances suggested for the "reining" were wooden spoons, spatulas, and green switches.

"Don't worry," they said. "A few swift swats, and he'll be toeing the line for sure!"

They meant well—but they were wrong. They had no idea (nor did I at the time) that I possessed so little control over my actions. So God grieved as I heeded misguided counsel and physically abused my son.

My utensil of choice was a green switch, and the awful truth is that I seldom used that switch in a calm and reasonable manner. Very rarely did I use that dumb green switch for anything but venting my own frustration over something Ricky Neal had said or done. I simply used that switch to get back at my son and to hurt him.

How I hate remembering those days. How I wish I would have thrown that awful thing in the yard and walked away! How I wish someone would have told me, "Julie, what you are doing is excessive—you must stop!"

As for his straightening up and toeing the line? Well, I did notice some subtle changes in the way he responded to me. He jumped a little quicker, and he argued with me a little less, but I grieved at the cost. I sensed a hardening of my son's spirit that was unnatural and dangerous. One experience tells it all.

TimeOut/Tamer: Make a policy—refuse to use any object against your child in a fit of anger or rage. Throw away any objects you've used in the past.

Ricky Neal was about five years old and was playing in our basement with his best friend, Colin, and his sister, Kristen, while I baked chocolate-chip cookies. A cool breeze ruffled the red gingham curtains over my kitchen window; I heard my four-month-old son, Patrick, awaking from his long afternoon nap. I was just coming back into the kitchen with Patrick on my hip when the front doorbell began ringing insistently.

I walked onto my front porch to see the county sheriff looking nervously through the screen door. "Are you all right, ma'am?"

"Huh...yes," was my reply.

He didn't look convinced. He asked if he could step in, and as we walked into the foyer he explained, "We just received a 9-1-1 phone call from this number. Our service identifies the calls as they come in, but when the operator tried to speak to the caller he hung up. She attempted to phone back to ensure that everything was all right, and the phone is off the hook. I just drove here at 75 miles per hour to make sure everything is okay."

That's when it dawned on me. I knew who had made that call—and this time, by gosh, maybe I'd let someone else put a little fear of God into the perpetrator.

"Officer, would you follow me downstairs, please? There's someone I'd like you to meet."

I walked ahead of him. As I descended the stairs, I heard little feet scurrying here and there, and caught a glimpse of a child hidden behind a plastic art easel. As I reached the bottom and looked back up behind me, I could see exactly what the hidden children saw.

A pair of shiny black boots clumped down the steps. Then, a pair of starched khaki pants and a gun holster—with gun!—came into sight. Finally, the sheriff stood in front of all of us—badge shining and eyes boring into the corners of the room.

"All right!" he commanded. "You kids show yourselves right now!"

Colin made his way from behind the easel. Ricky Neal popped out from behind a large piece of plywood while Kristen emerged quietly from the side of the room.

The sheriff announced in a controlled voice, just above a whisper, "I'm going to ask you *one* time…who called 9-1-1?" Two pointer fingers nailed Ricky as the culprit. There is no sibling loyalty when a county sheriff is involved! The sheriff asked Ricky to step forward and bent over to speak to him.

This is the point where most children would have wet their pants. I mean, really! You're four years old, and an armed officer of the law is staring at you like you were a buck caught in his sights!

But not my Ricky Neal. He stood ramrod straight and never blinked an eye or shed a tear. Even after the sheriff took him into the backseat of the police car and shut the door for a few moments, he walked back to the house with the same hard expression and never uttered a sound.

I had asked the sheriff to teach Ricky a lesson, but I'm the one who truly learned something that day. I saw, for the first time, that my son's spirit had begun hardening toward authority, and I knew the hardening was in no small part because of the way I had treated him physically. I found myself nose to nose with the reality that I really had gone too far, that my actions and attitudes had crossed the line into actual abuse. I'm clearly not the only one who has done this. Let's face some uncomfortable yet necessary facts:

> If statistics are correct, "every sixty seconds a child is abused….[and] more than seven hundred children are killed by their own parents each year." Consequently, child abuse has become the fifth most common cause of child death in the U.S. And, the average age of an abused child is less than three years old.[3]

Of those 700 childhood deaths, will we admit the distinct possibility that some of them occurred in families claiming Jesus Christ as their Lord? Isn't it possible that some of those 700 families showed no outward signs of the abuse that was going on?

Will we admit that of those 700 families there were some at which relatives, friends, and pastors gasped in disbelief when they learned the hidden truth about a parent's shame and abuse? Are we so foolish as to think the body of Christ is immune to the tensions of family life and the resulting behaviors of physical abuse?

It's time to get real and ask ourselves: *Have I gone too far? Have I physically abused my child?*

TimeOut/Tamer: Many mothers have "unspeakable feelings" about their children; however, if you find yourself struggling with homicidal urges—or if you fear you're losing control—seek professional counsel immediately! You can speak with a trained counselor at the National Child Abuse Hotline at 1-800-422-4453.

Real Mom Points to Ponder

Have you gone too far physically when dealing with your child? The following questions might help you decide.

1. Has your child ever sustained a physical injury from your actions toward him or her? (Think about bleeding welts from an instrument of discipline, any bruising or pinch marks left as a result of squeezing a child's tender skin.) Have you ever bitten your child—most likely in the early toddler stages—in hopes of showing him how much it hurts? What about goose eggs on the forehead from being shoved or pushed violently? Has your child suffered broken bones or been put in a harmful position as a result of your physical actions? (Think about my story of throwing Kristen. She may have escaped actual physical harm, but my throwing her was improper and excessive…it was abuse, plain and simple.)

2. Have you ever overdisciplined and caused physical injury to your toddler, preschooler, or older elementary-age child? Maybe the child moved or tried to avoid the physical punishment to come, and that enraged you all the more. As a result, you may have paddled too hard or for too long so you could vent your emotions of

anger and frustration. Were you physically spent after such an occurrence?

3. Have you ever kept your children from church nurseries, playgroups, or classroom situations to avoid questions from adult staff members or volunteer parents concerning marks on your child? If that child were able to articulate what had happened, would you feel uncomfortable and worry about others hearing it?

4. Have you ever admitted *to yourself* that you have been physically abusive? Have you ever shared this with anyone else in hope of finding change for your life?

Emotional Abuse: Invisible Yet Deadly

Not all abuse of children is physical, of course. Some of the most harmful forms of abuse can occur without a hand being laid on a child. A parent, who has such influence on a child, has astonishing power to bruise that child's tender feelings, to injure his self-esteem, to stunt his emotional growth with words and actions.

While there is no universally accepted definition of emotional abuse, I believe it is best described in summary as "either a neglect [of] or assault on a child's mind and emotional needs."[4] Emotional abuse often means playing mind games of some sort. Four common manifestations of emotional abuse are:

- *Rejecting*—repeatedly treating a child in a way that suggests resentment, rejection, or dislike

- *Degrading*—insulting, ridiculing, name calling, and imitating in a way that diminishes the identity, dignity, and self-worth of the child

- *Terrorizing*—inducing terror or extreme fear; threatening to destroy a child's possessions; threatening to leave or physically hurt a child

- *Denying emotional responsiveness*—failing to provide care in a sensitive and responsive manner; being detached and uninvolved; ignoring a child's attempt to interact; failing to show affection, care or love for a child

TimeOut/Tamer: "The wise woman builds her house, but the foolish tears it down with her own hands" (Proverbs 14:1). *Or with her own mouth!*

In the following pages I am emphasizing the verbal forms of emotional abuse because I believe our mouths—or better said, our tongues—can be the most destructive weapon we possess as mothers. It is so easy to spout off verbal attacks on our children and to do so with hardly a thought. In the area of emotional abuse, it is often our words that need to be most carefully weighed.

Here are some of the most common forms of verbal abuse! Do any of them sound familiar?

- *Belittling* (saying things that cause another person to seem little or lesser):

    "Can't you button that coat right? You never get the buttons lined up with the holes."

    "I can't believe you did that with your hair! You look like an idiot."

    "When are you going to learn to throw a decent pitch? Maybe if you had some halfway decent muscles, you'd do better."

- *Name-calling* (using offensive names, especially to win an argument or to communicate rejection or condemnation without objective consideration of the facts):

  "Only a complete dummy would fail to pass that test."

  "I've never seen such a useless kid."

  "Close your mouth and quit acting like such a dork."

  "You were such a mistake."

- *Comparing* (suggesting that one person doesn't measure up to another):

  "Why can't you be more like your...?"

  "I never had as much trouble with..."

- *Cursing* (using flat-out profanity or one of those "Christianized" phrases that carry the same suffocating weight):

  (Do I really need to illustrate this one?)

- *Shaming* (implying that the other person is essentially unworthy of love):

  "I don't even want people to know you're my kid!"

  "You're just no good."

- *Threatening* (implying physical violence):

  "I'd like to wring your neck."

  "I ought to smack you silly."

- *Guilt* (manipulating by accusing a person of malice):

  "How could you do this to me?"

  "I guess you like hurting your little brother."

- *Negative predictions* (making verbal comments—marked by hostility, withdrawal, or pessimism—that hinder or oppose constructive response or development):

    "You will never amount to anything!"

    "You'll disappoint us just like your sister did."

    "You'll never change."

    "Why bother trying? You'll probably mess it up like always."

- *Scapegoating* (blaming others for one's mistakes and failures):

    "I wouldn't have to yell so much if you kids would just act halfway decent!"

    "You're the only reason I'm stuck at home/working full-time/single/miserable/out of control!"

TimeOut/Tamer: Remember the words of Charlie Brown's teacher—"Wha-wha-wha, wha-wha-wha-wha"? Consider: Your children hear nothing more than this when you froth and fume during a verbal tirade. So when you become aware that you are about to spew verbal magma, clamp your mouth shut and *do not speak!* If necessary, put your hand over your mouth and scream through it, but *do not utter a word* until you have gained a measure of control.

Other Kinds of Invisible Abuse

While verbal punishment is the most common form of emotional abuse moms indulge in, we should be aware that there are other ways to bruise a child emotionally. Any form of physical abuse, for instance, does emotional damage as well. Mothers who create a climate of fear and hostility for a child through bullying or oppression are certainly guilty of emotional abuse. So are mothers who fail to acknowledge a child's worth and recognize his or her accomplishments. And mothers who distance themselves physically or emotionally from their children are practicing a subtle but damaging form of emotional abuse often referred to as "emotional neglect."

During the peak of my *She's Gonna Blow!* season, I did this with my own children. Oh, I was there in body, but I closed off the deeper emotions of my mothering heart and treated my children in a distant, clinical manner. Oddly enough, I really meant well in doing this. I *knew* my fiery anger was out of control and damaging, so I reasoned (with as much reason as an overstressed, hurting, confused mother can muster) that a detached demeanor would save me. At the time, it seemed to be the only way to avoid a complete nervous breakdown.

TimeOut/Tamer: If you're like me, it's the unexpected that always throws you for a loop and triggers the response of anger. The trouble is, if you have children there will always be something that comes up...or out...unexpectedly! Taking a few minutes to plan can do a lot to prevent angry eruptions. For instance, you can keep a plastic container in the back of your van or car that holds extra diapers and wipes, spare clothes for each child, a spare T-shirt for Mom and Dad, and snacks that travel well in a plastic bag.

If it hadn't been for the grace of God and a timely chapter in a book about "Siberian" (cold, distant, and destructive) parenting—*Love and Power*—by Dr. Glenn Austin—I would have continued on this disastrous course. Thank God I was able to recognize my abusive mentality enough to cry out to Him and lean on His love and care as He restored to me a heart for my children.

Another common form of emotional abuse is something I call "roller-coaster parenting." Kristen and Ricky took more than one harrowing trip with their mother on this stomach-churning parenting ride—with me lurching dizzily from rigid discipline to lax inattention to guilty smothering, whizzing along at the whim of my own changing emotions. Here's a typical scenario from my early parenting days.

Everything seems okay when we awake in the morning. Kristen is now eating her bowl of Cheerios, and Ricky Neal is happily smearing his face with apple and cinnamon oatmeal while I load the washing machine and try to engage in a halfway understandable conversation with the two.

Then it happens. The phone rings and diverts my attention for the briefest instant—during which the oatmeal finds its way to the light on the ceiling and Kristen presents her baby brother with a bite mark worthy of a cougar. Ricky howls with pain. Kristen scoots into the living room. And Mother yells.

"Kristen Jean Barnhill! You get back in this kitchen right now!"

She doesn't. She won't.

"Kristen Jean Barnhill! Get in this room before I come in there and make you wish you had."

Nope. Not going to do it.

I stomp into the living room—and a red Lego block imbeds itself permanently in the arch of my left foot. Then I lose it—scream, yell, grab Kristen, handle her much too roughly. I march her into her room, plop her on her bed, and tell her what a mean little girl she is for biting her baby brother. She begins to cry and I glare at her, walk away, and slam the door behind me.

But then, as her tiny sobs penetrate my angry, out-of-control heart, I begin to feel guilty. Very guilty. Oh, why did I react so violently? Why couldn't I just deal with it without acting like a complete fool? Why did I call *her* mean and hateful?

Taking Ricky Neal out of his high chair, I carry him to Kristen's room and kneel down beside her and sob. "Kristen, Mommy is so sorry she was so mean. Mommy isn't very nice sometimes. Will you forgive me?"

Kristen looks at me as if to say, "What is with you?" Yet each time we play out this crazy scenario, she wraps her tiny arms around my neck, gives me a kiss, and pats me on the back as if to say, "Poor Mommy."

More crying from me.

More confusion for Kristen and Ricky.

A roller coaster indeed. Hot one minute, cold the next, disciplining with control one moment, berating and punishing the next—from one extreme to the other. In retrospect, I have come to see this as a form of emotional abuse.

Once again, it was not intentional, just a result of my out-of-control emotions. But isn't that true of most maternal explosions? Even with the best intentions, our emotions get the best of us. That's why it's so important to explore the reasons for our past explosions and also to think ahead toward strategies to prevent future ones.

Emotional abuse is an elusive subject, and few experts agree on every aspect of it. There's no question, however, that emotional abuse is a painful reality in the lives of many families, and we would do well to root it out of our lives, trusting God as we try to replace it with gentle words, acts of kindness, and loving self-sacrifice.

Real Mom Points to Ponder

Have you gone too far emotionally when dealing with your child? The following questions might help you decide.

1. Listen to your children speak around their friends. Do they belittle their own abilities or themselves? Are they perhaps parroting the jibes and put-downs that you have spoken?

2. Have you ever heard your kids using the kind of language described in the preceding pages? Are they "verbal bullies"? If so, where do you think they learned this language?

3. What's the difference between backing off—putting distance between you and a stressful situation—and withdrawing emotionally from a child?

4. Have you ever overcompensated after an emotional outburst toward your children—plying them with treats to make up for your inappropriate behavior? What do think would be a more positive approach?

5. What abusive words or phrases do you need to remove from your vocabulary? Think of any accompanying body language that needs to be stopped as well. What are some positive verbal alternatives to use in the kinds of situations explained above?

Spiritual Abuse

Spiritual abuse is the misuse or neglect or both of the parental authority entrusted to us by our heavenly Father—especially the distortion of our children's perception of God and His holy character.

For better or worse, our children are observing us, listening both to what we say and to what is spoken by our silence. We are contractors, so to speak, helping to build up or tear apart the framework of their spirits, souls, and minds. The combination of our parental words, actions, and deeds will affect their perception of their heavenly Father—the Master Builder—over the course of their entire lives.

What an amazing responsibility this is—to teach our children about the Bible, about prayer, about loving service, and about God's character. And there are so many ways to do this—by taking them to church (and going with them), by holding family devotions, by reading the Bible with them and having them memorize Scripture, by including them in our acts of charity, by modeling for them a life of godly service. Because these forms of teaching are extremely important, neglecting them can truly be considered a form of spiritual abuse or neglect.

But our task as parents is not just to teach our children *about* God, but to model for them, to the best of our ability, what God *is like*. The Bible teaches us that God is kind, slow to anger, merciful, gracious, righteous, abounding in lovingkindness, a stronghold, a shield, a protector, a defender of the weak, perfect, sure, pure, true, gracious, strong, and good. And those are just a few of His incredible attributes! It is here that I have to ask myself, "Will my children be able to believe these truths about God as a result of their earthly mother's life and behavior?"

As mothers, we are the living, breathing, "in your face" examples of Christ to our children. By our uncontrolled anger, words, and actions, are we creating an image for our children of an out-of-control, impatient, and manipulative God? Will they be able to believe that God is merciful if we seldom demonstrate mercy toward them in their childishness? Will they *ever* be able to grasp the concept of grace— unmerited favor—if we as their mothers never extend grace to the "least of these"? Will they be able to believe there is forgiveness for *all* sin if we never confess our own and ask them to forgive us?

The book of Proverbs vividly summarizes the importance of a mother's words and example in the spiritual development of a child:

> Do not forsake the teaching of your mother; bind them continually on your heart; tie them around your neck. When you walk about, they will guide you; when you sleep, they will watch over you; and when you awake, they will talk to you (Proverbs 6:20-22).

What a marvelous goal to strive for in our relationship with our children. As they embark upon their own walk in life, they need the remembrance of both our words and our actions to guide them. Oh that the words and actions they remember would smooth their way and point them to a loving Creator!

Do you see how important this is? It's not that Junior will remember every little utterance and experience of his childhood, but that over the course of your time together he will recall your godly example and your words of encouragement and life! God forbid that we minimize the spiritual impact of our mothering—or the volcanic damage that spiritual abuse can do!

TimeOut/Tamers: Here is a prayer to use both daily and at times of stress to remind you of the spiritual impact of your mothering. You might want to write it on a card and keep it on the refrigerator or your makeup mirror.

"Dear Father: Open my eyes to the fact that I teach my child/children about You in the daily routines of our life. While we are in the car, traveling to and from school or practice, I am teaching them about You. Through my reactions to their failures and mistakes, I am teaching them about You. And dear God, in my furious outbursts or my silence and coldness, I am also teaching them about You. Teach me anew the spiritual significance of my life as a mom, and show me any abuses that I need to rid our lives of through Your grace and power. Amen."

Real Mom Points to Ponder

1. What lessons about God are your children learning by the way you treat them?

2. What are some areas of spiritual teaching that you tend to neglect with your children? What are some reasons for this?

3. Had you ever considered the concept of spiritual abuse before reading this chapter? If your children had your actions alone by which to create a belief system about God, what might their perspective be about His patience? His willingness to forgive? His ability to love unconditionally?

The God of the Volcano: The Ultimate Truth About Motherhood, God, Anger, and Abuse

As I struggled to pull all these bits and pieces of truth together for you, my reader, a friend made a wise observation. She wrote, "Many Christian moms feel guilty about being 'bad' mothers because they are angry with their children, but they don't always connect this anger with their sinfulness—and so they miss out on the remedy."

Well said!

The truth is, all our difficulties and struggles with our children have their roots in basic human sinfulness. And the only final and dependable solution to our *She's Gonna Blow!* dilemmas—whether minor or abusive—lies in our ongoing relationship with our own heavenly Father. Only as we ground our life in the solid bedrock of God's truth do we have any hope of turning fiery Mount Momma into something beautiful, nurturing, and inspiring. That's because only He has the answer to the human sinfulness that underlies all our problems with anger toward our children.

But please understand—I'm not saying that simply *being* angry or simply *feeling* that emotion is sinful. Anger is basically a God-given physical response to a perceived threat. It's part of the way we're made, and we can't help feeling it from time to time.

The sinfulness comes into play as we react—verbally, physically, or emotionally—in response to our emotion of anger. The apostle Paul exhorted us, "Be angry, and yet do not sin" (Ephesians 4:26). That means it really is possible to feel anger and even express anger without sinning. It's just *very* difficult to do, particularly with one's own child! Dr. Gary Chapman, noted author and nationally known speaker on family and marriage, says this about God's design and purpose for the emotion of anger:

> God experiences anger when He encounters evil. We reflect God's image and also experience anger when we encounter what we perceive to be wrong. Thus what is God's purpose for our

anger? I believe the answer is clear: Human anger is designed of God to motivate us to take constructive action in the face of wrongdoing or injustice.

Anger is not designed to stimulate us to do destructive things to the people who have wronged us. Anger's fundamental purpose is to motivate us to positive, loving action that will leave things better than we found them.[5]

There's the rub, of course! We can't stop ourselves from feeling anger, even toward our children. But we *must* learn to deal with this anger in such a way that our relationships with our children, our ability to communicate with them, and the positive tone of our homes is preserved and even improved. If we don't—if we let our anger control us and harm our relationship with our children—then we have sinned!

This is so important to recognize, especially when we are talking about the sticky issue of abuse. It's so easy to think of "child abusers" as monsters—certainly not like anyone we know, certainly not like us, most certainly not like us Christians! No wonder we shrink from acknowledging the damage we do to our children with our excessive and out-of-control behavior.

But when we face the reality that uncontrolled anger toward our children, even anger that expresses itself as abuse, is a sin no better but *not necessarily worse* than other sins, everything looks different.

In the fifth chapter of Galatians, Paul points out several to-be-avoided "deeds of the flesh," actions that work in direct opposition to the Holy Spirit in our lives. He starts with a few biggies like impurity, idolatry, and sorcery and progresses on toward those that make me feel a bit uncomfortable—like jealousy and strife.

And then, right there in the middle, I read the following: "outbursts of anger." Yikes! You mean God looks at bowing to an idol and my uncontrolled outbursts of anger in the same light? It appears to be so. But this deed of the flesh, like all other sins, has a remedy that is spelled out clearly in God's word: confession, forgiveness, true repentance, and a renewing of the mind.

God is so big and so...well, so *God* that He can change everything about us if we invite Him to do so. We need to remind ourselves continually of these incredible truths, which we will explore more in the coming chapters. In the meantime, if you are worried because you've identified with some of the words and actions identified in this subject, take heart.

Abuse, like sin, is serious business. But sin, in God's scheme of things, never has the last word. And that's the word of hope I want you to hold on to as we begin to focus on the practical strategies that will enable you to climb back to mothering with joy and sanity.

Real Mom Points to Ponder

Somehow, in ways I cannot begin to comprehend, God is able to bring healing to our souls through His written Word. In chapter six we will look at this reality in more detail. In the meantime, meditate upon the following passages and consider what they might mean to you regarding your anger toward your children.

1. "[She] who is slow to anger has great understanding, but [she] who is quick-tempered exalts folly" (Proverbs 14:29).

2. "Be angry, and yet do not sin; do not let the sun go down on your anger, and do not give the devil an opportunity" (Ephesians 4:26,27).

3. "Confess your sins to one another, and pray for one another so that you may be healed. The effective prayer of a righteous [woman] can accomplish much" (James 5:16).

4. "Do not be conformed to this world, but be transformed by the renewing of your mind, so that you may prove what the will of God is, that which is good and acceptable and perfect" (Romans 12:2).

5. "If we say that we have no sin, we are deceiving ourselves and the truth is not in us. If we confess our sins, He is faithful and righteous to forgive us our sins and to cleanse us from all unrighteousness" (1 John 1:8,9).

6. "They were even more astonished and said to Him, 'Then who can be saved?' Looking at them, Jesus said, 'With people it is impossible, but not with God; for all things are possible with God' " (Mark 10:26,27).

Part Two

Climbing
to Sanity

The Bedrock of Truth

Exploring the Biblical Foundations for Change

Bedrock.

That's the name geologists give to the solid surface of the earth's crust, the hard rock that underlies all the loose sand and soil and gravel. Engineers like to anchor their structures to the bedrock because it's a solid, sure foundation. The very word itself has come to mean "solid, sure, dependable."

It's the very opposite of seething, excitable, miserable Mount Momma.

And that's what I think we need to look for when it comes to dealing with our anger and angry behavior toward our children.

Yes, it's important to understand where it all comes from and how it happens. That's what we've been doing in the preceding chapters.

And yes, it helps to develop practical strategies for changing. We've done a little of that, too, and we'll do a lot of it in the last chapter.

But in order to make real, lasting changes in our parenting style, to convert our angry rages to peaceful, purposeful parenting, we need to do more than understand. We need more than quick fixes and gimmicks or even practical rebuilding strategies.

In order to really change, we need to pay some attention to the very foundation of our being. We need to anchor both our lives and our parenting styles on something solid.

Something strong—bedrock strong.

But not just any old bedrock will do!

Here on earth, after all, as our mini-study of volcanoes has made clear, even the rock beneath our feet can be less than solid. Here on earth the most solid rock can shift or crack…and unleash unspeakable things from down below.

That's why I think we need to ground our parenting on bedrock truths that are even more solid than the solid rock beneath us—and much more solid than our personal ideals, our best intentions, and our strongest determination.

Where can we find that kind of solid, dependable foundation?

I think you know the answer—even if you haven't had time to read it lately…

Read a "Good" Book Lately?

When I die, I have asked Rick to have the following engraved upon my tombstone, "I just read the *best* book!"

I have always loved to read—even back when I couldn't read at all. My mother tells me that as a three- and four-year-old child I would sit for hours and listen to her read. I was always the first one to attend story hour at our public library, and I would sit there completely mesmerized as Geraldine and Cynthia regaled us with the fantastic adventures of the Boxcar Children and Pippi Longstocking.

(Two years ago I read the original Boxcar book aloud to my children. They moaned and groaned when they saw the "old" cover and complained that it would be "boring." Well, that lasted about one chapter. Soon they were caught up in the tender story, and each had taken a character name for himself or herself. "Henry, Violet, and Benny" Barnhill were soon foraging for blueberries at our local grocery store and putting together straw brooms with twine and twigs!)

As a young teenager I read *Tiger Beat* magazine and tried to choose between Jay or Donnie Osmond as my future groom. A few years later, I was grabbing the latest *Seventeen*, *Glamour*, or *Teen* periodical and discovering new products to lengthen my lashes, cleanse my complexion, and bring the boys running. I recall reading a *Cosmopolitan* magazine while waiting for my mother to have her hair done at Marion's Beauty Shop. I hid it behind the open pages of a *Capper's Weekly Newspaper* and read it with an appropriately bug-eyed expression, I'm sure!

And I cannot forget the workhorse magazine of all pop culture and the staple of my early adult life...*People* magazine. I read it religiously and could rattle off the marital and mental stability of most any movie star ever featured. Years ago, after one particular game of Trivial Pursuit in which I had decimated my husband with my repertoire of trivial knowledge, he bowed in humble adoration and remarked, "Julie, you know more about nothing than anyone I know." And he was right. I had managed to fill my brain with fluff and little substance. No wonder that, when the struggles of early motherhood upended my world, I found myself drowning, desperately longing for a lifeline to grab on to.

Many of our decisions as mothers are motivated and determined by the things we have digested within our culture, be they books, magazines, soap operas, or network television. That's why it is imperative that we align our hearts and minds with the bedrock truth of God's Word. That truth is the only thing that will ultimately save us in our struggles as mothers and as women. And the way to stay close to that truth, of course, is to spend significant time in the Good Book.

I'm not saying it's an easy thing to do—this goal of reading and studying the Bible in the middle of motherhood. I would guess that your first inclination is to read anything *but* the Bible. I understand, trust me...at one time I had more than ten magazine subscriptions and probably picked up that many more off the rack while waiting in line at the grocery store! I was an information junkie, craving empty calories of junk-food trivia. It was much easier to grab a dose of *Regis and Kathie Lee* in between morning baby naps than to discipline myself and study the Word of God.

But I've learned the hard way that it is simply impossible to grow in the faith if the only source you're tapping into is cultural junk food and your biblical past.

You may have memorized the books of the Bible during Vacation Bible School in 1972, but you are going to need a fresh encounter with Holy Scripture for today—and for every day.

You may have agonized over Greek meanings and biblical context in a college class, but you are going to need a fresh encounter with the living Word for today—and for every day.

If we want lasting change in our hearts and in our family relationships, if we want to build our lives on a rock-solid foundation, then we must reacquaint ourselves with the Word of God and discover anew the truths it has to tell us about God, about ourselves, about our children, and about what it means to be a good mother.

TimeOut/Tamers: Here are a few of the Bible's "SOS passages"—words of comfort and encouragement from God's Word to give you a boost in your fatigued, stressful, about-to-blow-it moments;

"Come to Me, all [moms] who are weary and heavy-laden, and I will give you rest" (Matthew 11:28).

"After you [moms] have suffered for a little while, the God of all grace, who called you to His eternal glory in Christ, will Himself perfect, confirm, strengthen and establish you" (1 Peter 5:10).

"Let us not lose heart in doing good, for in due time we will reap if we do not grow weary" (Galatians 6:9).

"He will feed His flock like a shepherd; He will gather the lambs [your children] with His arm, and carry them in His bosom, and gently lead those who are with young [you!]" (Isaiah 40:11 NKJV).

The Truth About Who God Is... and Who We Are

"From a Distance." That was the title of a song made popular several years ago by Bette Midler. The lyrics hinted that God was off somewhere, watching us from afar as we messed up our lives.

It was a pretty good song. The trouble is, it just wasn't true—it's a completely different picture of God than the one we see in the Bible! He's not a distant, sneering, unconcerned deity. Rather, He's as near as the breath you last breathed, as near as the thoughts you've yet to complete. In fact, the Bible teaches that He knew our thoughts before we were even created. Imagine that!

The God of the Bible is a personal Creator, not an impersonal force mixed in with random chance and circumstance. He made us, and He loves us with the love of the tenderest, most protective of parents. The God of Abraham, Isaac, and Jacob does not grow weary or tired—unlike you and me, who nod off during *Rugrats.* Our Father God never sleeps, and nothing ever catches Him off guard. This God has known of your struggles and mine, the battles we fight as mothers, since long before time came to exist!

TimeOut/Tamer: Just a reminder: God the Father knows how to "mother" us too! "Can a woman forget her nursing child and have no compassion on the son of her womb? Even these may forget, but I will not forget you. Behold, I have inscribed you on the palms of My hands" (Isaiah 49:15,16).

How marvelous are these truths about our faithful and loving God! We can entrust ourselves completely to Him who knows us more intimately than we know ourselves. The more we learn to lean on Him and learn from Him, the more our anger will take its proper place and our parenting will come to follow His example of tender mercy, loving discipline, and positive guidance.

But what about us? What does the Bible say about our humanity—and our mothering role—in the light of God's glory?

Well, the good news is that we're created in His image. The very fingerprints of God are on our spirits, our souls, and our minds. Right after God created Eve, He declared that His creation was good—and that means you and I have been declared a good thing also. We were created to worship and enjoy our heavenly Father. We were created to know Him and to find eternal fulfillment through His Son Jesus Christ. That's the good news about our humanity.

The not-so-good news is that we humans are part of a fallen creation, which means that our hearts are desperately wicked and prone to sin and destruction. It is our human nature to sin—and to do so time and time again! We all have the capacity to turn a good thing—even our mothering love—into something terrible. By ourselves, we just can't change our core nature—this includes all humanity, male and female alike—from being selfish, cunning, sinful, and spiritually lost.

What that means, in practical terms, is that without God, we don't have a prayer of permanently changing our angry behavior toward our children. Without God, all our attempts to calm down, cool down, and treat our children differently will be doomed to failure. Without God, when the pressure builds, our natural reaction will be to take it out on the least powerful people in sight—our children, the very ones that God has entrusted to us.

But here's some more good news: God really can change us.

God alone can change our nature. Only the God who created us has the power to take hearts that are cold and hard and make them soft and pliable. Only a Creator who gave His only Son for us can give us a heart for our own children.

If you are a believer in Christ, the promise of how it can happen is found in 1 John 1:9: "If we confess our sins, He is faithful and righteous to forgive us our sins and to cleanse us from all unrighteousness."

If you have not yet confessed Christ as Savior, your promise is found in the book of Romans, chapter 10, verses 9-11:

> If you confess with your mouth Jesus as Lord, and believe in your heart that God raised Him from the dead, you will be saved; for with the heart a person believes, resulting in righteousness, and with the mouth he confesses, resulting in salvation. For the Scripture says, "Whoever believes in Him will not be disappointed."

Making a Beginning

This is where it has to start—with true repentance for our sins of anger and abuse. It begins with looking clearly at what we've become and saying, "No more. I'm sorry. I don't want to do this again."

We're not talking about a promise to "do better next time"—we *all* know what happens to those kinds of promises! What we're really talking about is facing the facts about how we're living, how destructive it is, and how much we want to change it—and then coming to the Lord to ask His help with all of this. The simple truth is that the Lord can't help us change if we insist on living in denial about what we're doing to ourselves and our children.

Repentance in turn must lead us to confession—to the Lord and perhaps to another person as well. We need to get our sins—including our mothering sins—out on the table where we can see them and specifically ask forgiveness for them.

And what comes next is possibly the hardest thing we have to do. We have to take God at His word that we *are* forgiven. We have to leave the guilt behind (because mounting guilt is just another cause of mothering stress) and walk forward in our everyday lives as mothers, trusting that God has set us free and that all we need to do is learn to live in that freedom.

And it's then that the change really begins. As we continue to spend time with the Lord, to spend time in His Word, we gradually start to see things differently—and that change in vision affects the way we act, too. The Bible calls this process the renewing of our minds. This type of renewal literally means "the adjustment of our moral and spiritual vision and thinking to conform to the very mind of God, which is designed to have a transforming effect upon your life"![1]

It means that we stop seeing things the way our culture says they should be—or even the way *we* think they should be—and start looking at our lives from God's point of view. In the process, we also continually find ourselves a little more grounded, a little more peaceful, perhaps a little less ready to blow.

It doesn't happen overnight. It doesn't always involve "aha!" moments or dramatic changes. But it's real…and powerful. The more we spend time in God's Word—both studying with our minds and listening with our hearts—the closer we come to being the kind of mothers God intends for us to be.

TimeOut/Tamer: Don't be embarrassed to turn to God in moments of maternal desperation—even the ones that seem a little silly. The God who loves you *does* care about spilt milk, and He especially cares about your reaction to it. When you feel the steam beginning to come out of your ears, try the "freeze and pray" method: Stop everything and throw up a prayer for patience and wisdom before you react.

Real Mom Points to Ponder

1. How close have you felt to God in recent months or years? Can you see any correlation between your parenting style and your relationship with your heavenly Father?

2. Have you actually asked God's forgiveness for your sins as a mother? Have you found it difficult to accept that forgiveness?

3. What do you do when you have gone to God and asked forgiveness—and you still have a problem with anger toward your children?

The Truth About Children

"Behold, children are a gift of the LORD; the fruit of the womb is a reward" (Psalm 127:3).

This is the basic truth about children that the Bible has to offer us.

Children are blessings. They aren't some cosmic mistake sent by happenstance from a hapless "Man Upstairs." And above all...children are not burdens, something to be endured for a season until we can get on with our lives.

Well, you knew that. But the challenge lies in remembering and *living* this truth in the midst of spit-up and diapers, scraped knees and squabbles, or pre-teens and hormones (theirs and ours!).

Contrast the verse from the book of Psalms with this quote I found in the reader opinion section in an issue of *Time* magazine: "This hoopla over the McCaughey septuplets is beyond me! It was bad enough to keep women barefoot and pregnant; now they have litters."[2]

I've often wished that the writer of this opinion had filled us in on a few details. Was she a mother of children? Did she have more than one?

I wonder, because I don't think this woman was simply railing against fertility drugs and procedures. If you re-read the quotation, I think you will see the real issue lies in her words "it was bad enough." What she seemed to be saying—and not so subtly—is that children are burdens. Just having children is a bad idea; it's an even worse idea when seven are involved.

It seems this woman has completely lost sight of the blessings of children and parenthood, and she isn't alone. Several years ago, roughly 50,000 parents responded to a query from advice columnist Ann Landers. She asked whether, if given the choice again, they would have children. A full 70 percent said no, that it just wasn't worth it—emotionally or financially. The financial burden children impose, the emotional wear and tear of raising them, the toll on marital relationships, the sacrifice of individual choices, and the parents' overall disappointment in their children as adults were all factors that were cited by the respondents.

Culturally, as the family has been transformed from a unit of production (pre–Industrial Revolution) to a unit of consumption, children have come to be viewed as economic liabilities rather than as assets. And it should come as no surprise that a price tag has been affixed to having children. According to the U.S. Department of Agriculture, the projected cost of raising a child born in 1999 through the age of 17 (not counting college) will range from $117,390 to $233,850.[3]

Surely that's where some of the "just not worth it" mentality comes into play. Most of us, if we would truly admit it, want—*expect*—something in return. In our materialistic society, it's all too easy to look for the bottom line and wonder whether we are getting an adequate return on our investment.

Subconsciously we may also expect our children to fulfill us—to make up for that which is lacking emotionally in our lives. We may expect to gain—upon their arrival—an overwhelming sense of purpose that has eluded us in years past. We may expect from them—upon their growing and maturing—a sense of gratitude for all the sacrifices we made on their behalf. And when these expectations are unmet, a nagging sense of failure can quickly undermine the pleasures of parenthood and leave one responding to an advice columnist: "It was bad enough the first time. I'd never do it again!"

That's why we all need to be reminded, sometimes again and again, that God's values are different from the values of our culture. God's values are not based on the bottom line or on personal satisfaction. We *all* need to be reminded of the sacredness of our children's lives and our sacred calling as their mothers—and once again, that is best accomplished by spending regular time in the Word of God, absorbing His values and learning to think the way He thinks.

Real Mom Points to Ponder

1. Under what circumstances do you tend to fall into the trap of thinking "children are burdens"? What faulty expectations on your part might have led to this thinking?

2. What do the following verses have to say about the way God views children?

   • "He makes the barren woman abide in the house as a joyful mother of children. Praise the LORD!" (Psalm 113:9).

- "Behold, children are a gift of the LORD, the fruit of the womb is a reward" (Psalm 127:3).

- "Grandchildren are the crown of old [women], and the glory of [children] is their [parents]"(Proverbs 17:6).

- "Whoever receives one such child in My name receives Me" (Matthew 18:5).

- "Be imitators of God, as beloved children" (Ephesians 5:1).

3. In light of the preceding verses (and any more you can find), what specific blessings does the Bible indicate that you can reasonably expect from your children?

4. In what ways can children who disappoint you end up being a blessing from God's point of view?

TimeOut/Tamer: In what specific ways can you see that your children have blessed your life? Tell them! Whisper one of these blessings to your newborn baby, sing one to your toddler, or write one on a note and slip it into your older child's school backpack. Write down these blessings in your journal, too—as a reminder for days when you begin to wonder. If you're like me, the more you express the fact that your children are blessings, the more you'll begin to believe it.

The Truth About "Good" Mothers

"I'm not a very good mother."

Ever said that about yourself? Maybe you're more prone to say, "I wish I was as good a mother as..."

I wish I could wave a magic wand and make the term "good mother" disappear forever. Not because it's wrong for us to want to be the very best we can be, but because I believe we as mothers have allowed ourselves to be sidetracked by an impossible standard of "good." More important, I think we have missed the essence of what God has to say about what kind of mothers *He* wants us to be.

After all, what is the picture of a good mother that tends to lurk in your (envious and discouraged) mind? Mine looks a little like this. She is a woman who:

- never loses her temper
- *wants* to be with her children 24 hours a day, 7 days a week
- doesn't mind children grazing from her dinner plate or 12-ounce drink
- is able to maintain a serene sense of control as she travels five hours alone with the kids to see their grandparents
- maintains a fashionable wardrobe for her children on one income
- doesn't wig out when her carefully hoarded Fiestaware plates are broken
- feels nothing but a maternal glow from pregnancies 18 months or less apart
- gently but firmly tells her kids, "No," and they listen!
- breastfeeds forever, then feeds her children only nutritious food
- graciously hands out sugar-free Popsicles to the entire population of neighborhood children aged two through ten...and does it every day

- is 100 percent satisfied with her life 100 percent of the time—and never complains 99.9 percent of the time
- and, of course, never regrets…anything
- and never, ever, blows her top when the stresses of parenting build!

Sounds familiar, doesn't it? But wait, there's more! The "good" *Christian* mother is someone who:

- never wants to fake being sick on Sundays or church activity nights
- does daily devotions with her children…daily!
- keeps an up-to-date prayer calendar, constantly interceding not only for her own children, but for the children of her friends, her Sunday school class, and the missionaries of the week
- memorizes *new* Bible verses—even after having children
- is never even tempted to use inappropriate language in stressful situations
- never doubts or worries because she always trusts God
- might get depressed…but "gets over it" quickly
- never fights with her husband (or just fumes in the background)

You see the real problem, don't you? Good mothers like that just don't exist! They're all in our heads—but the pressure they exert on us can be all but unbearable! Sometimes, in fact, it's been this pressure alone that pushed my Mount Momma to the point of eruption.

We keep a checklist of mothering perfections, yet overlook one ironic fact—which is that God doesn't ever really call us to be "good mothers," at least not as we tend to define it. Instead, He calls us to love Him, to become more like Him—that is, to be "godly" mothers.

God Wants More than a "Good Mother"

We have two choices. We can keep trying in our own strength—and failing—to achieve whatever "good mother" standard we have accumulated in our heads. Or we can turn to God, admit that we're just not up to being good, and ask Him to teach us more about Himself.

In the process, we can be encouraged by such biblical examples as Lois and Eunice, the grandmother and mother of Timothy, the "beloved son" that the apostle Paul tutored and encouraged. In his letters to Timothy, Paul reminds his young pupil of the legacy of sincere faith that these two influential women bestowed upon him. In the third chapter of 2 Timothy, Paul makes this observation, "From childhood you have known the sacred writings which are able to give you the wisdom that leads to salvation through faith which is in Christ Jesus" (verse 15).

Now, who do you suppose taught Timothy those childhood truths? Who do you suppose taught him to read and discern the sacred writings? No mention is made of Timothy's father. No mention is made of a rabbi or priest. No, the only people mentioned in the book of 2 Timothy are Lois and Eunice: "I am mindful of the sincere faith within you, which first dwelt in your grandmother Lois and your mother Eunice, and I am sure that it is in you as well" (1:5).

It is crucially important to note that the thing Paul was commending in these two women was their personal faith in Christ Jesus. And Paul assumed with absolute confidence that this faith had naturally been lived out right in front of Timothy and was now a dynamic truth in his life as well.

Lois and Eunice had a personal relationship with Jesus Christ. They loved God and, as a result, Timothy was able to follow in the sincere faith these two precious and godly women demonstrated in their day-to-day lives as grandmother and mother.

And *that*, according to the Word of God, is the kind of mothering He wants out of us.

If you want more examples, you can study the Scriptures and learn about other mothers such as Jochebed, the mother of Moses; Hannah, the mother of Samuel; Sarah, the mother of Isaac; and of course Mary, the mother of Jesus! (Can you imagine! If any woman had a right to boast in her "good mothering" it would be Mary, but we read nothing of this in Scripture.)

Each of these women's stories bears out the same truth: It was their faith and trust in God (though weak and feeble at times) that made the difference. It was their faith that was important enough to be recorded for all eternity. These mothers trusted God in spite of infertility, old age, savage rulers, unfair laws and customs. These mothers loved God, and He loved them.

So here's the bedrock truth about our role as mothers that I think bears repeating again and again: God doesn't want us to be "good mothers"; He simply wants *us!* He wants us to be His children, to draw on His strength, to learn from Him what it means to be a successful human being.

But here's the interesting thing. As we draw closer to Him—learning about Him, depending on Him, allowing Him to handle the inevitable pressures in our lives, we'll become more godly women…His women.

And *then,* as a byproduct of this dynamic and personal relationship with Him, we may even find ourselves coming to resemble the good mother we had in mind to begin with.

No, we won't be perfect. Chances are we'll still blow it from time to time. But as we strive to be women of God, we will be growing more and more into the likeness of Christ, so that even our precious little ones can clearly see in us the face of the Father.

Who knows, they might even follow the example of the children in Proverbs 31.

They might rise up and bless us!

Real Mom Points to Ponder

1. What image of a "good mother" tends to rule in your head? List five things that this "good mother" does or doesn't do.

2. Use a good concordance or one of the online Bible study resources listed in the back of this book and begin a word study of the following: *children, blessing, good, godly,* and *mother.* Ask the Lord to show you any differences between your list of "good" things and His Word.

3. Think of three things you could do in the course of a day that would be likely to show your children the image of Christ. (Examples: forgive someone who has hurt you, speak softly instead of harshly, help someone who needs help.) Ask for God's help in actually doing at least one of these things in the next week.

The Truth About God's Lavish Grace

Changing the way you relate to your children is not a simple proposition—even with God's help. Chances are, you won't be transformed from a volatile Mount Momma into a patient, nurturing, rock-solid woman of God overnight. So much is involved—the ideas and assumptions you absorbed from culture, the things you were taught, the things you experienced as a child, the pressures you are under every day. It's going to take time, and it's going to take work, and it's definitely going to require a lot of help from your heavenly Father.

But that's where one of the best truths of all comes in—which is that God has promised to help us, and that God always keeps His promises.

Let's look at two of the most astounding of these promises toward us. Read each one through slowly as you ponder what it could mean in your life as a mother, especially as you try to change the ways you relate to your children:

- *Promise One:* "Now to Him who is able to do far more abundantly beyond all that we ask or think, according to the power that works within us, to Him be the glory in the church and in Christ Jesus to all generations forever and ever" (Ephesians 3:20, 21).

- *Promise Two:* "We have not ceased to pray for you and to ask that you may be filled with the knowledge of His will in all spiritual wisdom and understanding, so that you will walk in a manner worthy of the Lord, to please Him in all respects, bearing fruit in every good work and increasing in the knowledge of God; strengthened with all power, according to His glorious might, for the attaining of all steadfastness and patience; joyously giving thanks to the Father, who has qualified us to share in the inheritance of the saints in Light" (Colossians 1:9-12).

Whew! I love the book of Colossians. Paul puts it out there as plainly as can be: There is abundant life for us in Christ. For all of us, mothers included.

Don't you want a taste of that abundance? Wouldn't you like to have an abundance of patience, an abundance of steadfastness toward your family, and an abundance of joy in your life as a mother?

When *is* the last time you experienced joyful abundance—not the temporal "happiness" that comes as a result of Junior sitting on the potty consistently for three days or the "happiness" of zipping up a pair of long-forgotten jeans—but joy that wells from the deepest core of your being? Joy that cannot be dampened by temporal happenings but is dependent upon an everlasting relationship with Jesus Christ? "Joy inexpressible" as the apostle Peter writes—a joy that cannot be contained?

Instead of spewing verbal lava and angry ashes, wouldn't you love for your family life to be overflowing with unspeakable joy? That's exactly what God has promised for those of us who come to Him, take advantage of His remedy for sin, and draw close to Him on a moment-by-moment basis.

One of my very favorite verses about this abundance is found in the first chapter of Ephesians, tucked in between verse seven and verse nine. In his prayer that lists Christ's redemptive acts toward us, Paul states, "In Him we have redemption through His blood, the forgiveness of our trespasses, according to the riches of His grace *which He lavished upon us*" (verses 7,8, emphasis added).

Grace Heaped on Grace

Stop the train, because these five words ("which He lavished upon us") pack a ton of power and promise for the transformation of Mount Momma!

Lavished. What do you think of when you read that word? What immediately springs to my mind is the memory of my grandma's angel food cake with cream-cheese frosting. *Lavish* was a main description of everything my grandmother baked, especially angel food cakes! You didn't simply get a piece of store-bought cake with a dab of icing. You received a gargantuan slice of homemade, heavenly lightness—made with 13 egg whites—that was piled high with a delectable concoction of cream cheese and powdered sugar.

I have been told that some children's grandmothers ice a cake with the precision of a drill sergeant. Friends of mine have personally witnessed these grandmothers scraping the icing as thinly as possibly across a cooling devil's food cake and have then watched horrified as the mixing bowl and beaters were rinsed clean without one cleansing lick from the child watching. Can you believe that? It didn't happen with my grandma! She didn't so much "ice" a cake as "lavish" a cake with icing. She used two eight-ounce portions of cream cheese and bags of powdered sugar to create scads of icing. I remember her scooping the creamy white icing from the mixing bowl with a large serving spoon and plopping it upon the awaiting cake.

Plop!

Lavish.

Plop!

Lavish.

Until the cake quivered beneath the creamy weight.

But the *best* part was how she iced the "funnel" section of the angel food cake. Grandma would scoop up a healthy spoonful of icing and then plop it right on the edge of the funnel. The icing would slowly ooze over and fall into the center portion as she took a spoon and, with the rounded back edge, coated the inner part with a lavish dose.

As Grandma served this dessert, the plentiful icing would pool along the rim of the serving platter. Adult guests would consider swiping a fingerful of icing as an appetizer; I was six, so I did it without hesitation! And

Grandma was always generous about letting me clean up the bowls and beaters, too.

Grandma baked and served with lavish abandon. She did so for the enjoyment of those she was serving. And you know what, moms? Jesus Christ wants to *lavish* Himself upon our lives in the same way. He won't apply "just enough" to get us by. Instead, He will heap—He will *inundate*—our lives with the riches of His grace and pile upon our hearts mercy so plentiful that it overflows and pools.

So here's the place to start building your house on bedrock:

- Accept the lavish grace that God has extended toward you as a mother. He is fully aware of the crazy schedules, hectic mornings, and emotional ups and downs that you deal with daily.

- Accept His lavish grace toward your commitment to study His Word, even if you have to do it in itty-bitty, bite-size pieces.

- Accept His lavish grace during the three-minute sessions of Bible reading that you fit in between children's naps, lunch breaks at work, or mornings over a bagel and juice.

- Accept His lavish grace toward you when two of those three minutes were spent feeling guilty for not spending more time reading the Bible.

In addition, give some thought to using *lavish* as an action verb in your life as a mother. Let's lavish our children with hugs, kisses, and words of praise! Let's lavish our laughter and smiles upon the children God has placed in our lives. And let's lavish our grace toward one another as mothers, laying aside tired arguments that divide us and concentrating on that which unites us all…our love for our children and our relationship with them.

But remember, we don't have a prayer of doing any of this if we aren't spending time in the Word of God, soaking in the abundance of His love and mercy. If we want to feel the consistent reality of God's lavish love plopping down on us, we have to put ourselves there on the "plate"—and, as any mother knows, "plate" time isn't always easy to come by when we have children. In the next chapter we'll explore a number of practical ways for combining motherhood and time in the Word. Before we do that, though, it might be a good idea for us to back off and get a sense of the big picture, the whole purpose of our mothering.

TimeOut/Tamer: Teachers have long been in on the secret that we learn best what we teach to others—so one of the best ways to live close to the Word is to teach it to your children. Take advantage of quiet times, story times, even high-stress times to share what you know with your children. Get an age-appropriate Bible version or a child's devotional book, or just tell stories from memory. As you share the Word with your little ones, you'll be planting it deeper in your own heart as well. (Don't forget to pray together, too.)

Real Mom Points to Ponder

1. What kind of lavish loving would each of your children appreciate most? Verbal praise? Cuddly one-on-one time? Wild cheers at a sporting event? Set aside some time this week to begin putting lavish love into practice.

2. What kind of experiences in your own life help you feel the reality of God's lavish love? A hike in the

woods? A blissful sleep-late morning? A long phone call with your best friend? What simple changes could you make to have these experiences more?

3. Bake your favorite cake and make lots of icing! With each lick of the spoon or beater, encourage your children to name one of God's "lavish" blessings in their lives.

The Truth of Living... In the Light of Eternity

All too often, my eyes are fixed upon the temporal and insignificant realities of everyday life. I yell over the cliché of spilt milk, get bent out of shape over sticky floors, mumble and nag over outdated home decor, and go ballistic over sundry factors that just don't matter. And invariably, no matter how hard I try to keep the eternal in the forefront of my mind, I can't...until some crisis occurs and I am faced once again with the truth about what really matters.

One of these crises involved two of our main characters: Ricky Neal and myself.

The children and I were visiting with my parents over spring break. My mother was recovering from surgery and was unable to walk without the aid of a walker. I was trying to help her out as much as I could while we visited.

One particular evening, Kristen was watching Patrick as I prepared dinner, and Ricky Neal was helping his beloved Papa complete chores outside the house.

I was standing in the kitchen rinsing some vegetables and listening to Patrick play with his sister in the front room when the stillness of the evening was shattered. I heard my father yell—through closed doors and windows— "Here now! Leave him alone!" In the split-second that followed, a plaintive and terrible wail reached my ears. I'd never heard anything like that cry, and I knew something was horribly wrong.

My first thoughts were of my son.

"Oh, dear God," I screamed, running to the back patio door, "something's happened to Ricky Neal!" I lunged through the back door and saw my father running toward me, clutching Ricky to his side.

"The dog got ahold of him!" he choked out between sobs. I turned to look at my son, and I wanted to vomit and scream. All I could see, all anyone could have seen at that time, was the blood—the crimson blood that seemed to be pouring from his entire head. He was terrified and shrieking. I knew I had to calm down, because that is what moms do for their children even when they feel themselves falling apart.

I took Ricky in my arms. My father fetched a towel, and as I attempted to stanch the flow of blood, I saw for the first time how horribly torn up his scalp was. My father's normally docile retriever had ripped the flesh at the crown of Ricky's head and gashed an opening at least five inches long above his left ear.

"We have to call an ambulance," I barked at my father, and as he ran inside I felt myself beginning to lose it. I wanted my husband there to deal with this, but he was working a third-shift schedule more than five hours away. I caught myself crying and held Ricky closer to my side. I was worried. I couldn't stop the flow of blood, and although Ricky's cries had subsided a bit, his complexion was pasty white. I clutched him tighter in a crazy mother attempt to stave off the terrifying fears that were mounting in my heart.

Suddenly an angel of sorts appeared, packing a paramedic's bag and speaking with a calming voice of reason.

My dad had somehow tracked down Jamie Bowyer, a paramedic who lived two houses down the block. He was a few years older than me and had a son the same age as Ricky Neal.

Jamie immediately took control of the situation. He looked at Ricky's wounds and instructed me to apply more pressure.

I hesitated, afraid I would hurt my son even more.

"Julie!" he spoke crisply, "Press the towel firmly on his head, now!"

Ricky's cries increased with the pressure, and he twisted away from me, but I could not relent. With tears streaming down my own face, I held firm until my hands began to feel numb. I found myself coming unglued, and with each passing moment I sobbed louder until I was shaking with grief. Then, a gentle hand grasped mine holding the towel. Jamie smiled and said, "Julie, the bleeding has stopped; he's going to be okay." I lifted the towel from his dark hair and saw that, yes, the bleeding had subsided.

As Jamie washed the caked blood from Ricky Neal's hands, his shrill cries became mournful sobs of pain. As I drew him close against my bosom, my heart felt as though it was shattering in a million pieces. I had never hurt so much for my son as I did right then. I felt powerless, powerless to have stopped this tragedy and unable to stop his pain.

I rocked him in my arms as we were driven 50 miles to the nearest hospital. I prayed aloud, gently caressing his arms as I whispered, "Dear God, take away my son's hurt. Father, dull the nerves and help him sleep safely on our way. Oh, Abba! Father!! Be what I cannot be, do what I cannot do."

As we arrived at the emergency unit, a waiting doctor immediately placed Ricky beneath a bright examining light. I sat beside him, holding his hand and soothing him with my voice. Then Ricky spoke in a voice I could hardly discern: "I'm scared, Mommy." His beautiful brown eyes reflected my own fear lurking just beneath the surface.

"Ricky Neal, do you remember the song we sing when we are afraid?"

As he gazed at me—fear and panic ready to overwhelm his tender heart—I began, "'When I am afraid, I will trust in you, I will trust in you, I will trust in you…'"

He reached his hand out toward me and gently rubbed my cheek. With a quavering voice he joined in: "'When I am afraid, I will trust in you…in God whose word I praise.'"

God granted me the privilege of seeing the eternal in that cold, sterile emergency room, and in that moment He seared the word *eternity* upon my heart and eyes.

In the light of eternity, spilled juice doesn't matter, but loving relationships do.

In the light of eternity, what you keep isn't nearly as important as what you give.

In the light of eternity, I'd rather hold my children than an award for speaking or a royalty check—and the financial bottom line doesn't matter at all.

In the light of eternity…"I love you" means I would give anything to take the pain for you.

In the light of God's eternity…irritating children become irreplaceable blessings. That's the bedrock truth. And it's the ultimate key to transforming volatile Mount Mommas back into the loving, nurturing mothers we truly long to be.

Real Mom Points to Ponder

1. In the light of eternity…what matters to *you?* Write that eternity truth in the form of a statement that you can place in a highly visible place in your home (your

bathroom mirror, perhaps, or the refrigerator door, or your computer screen). Each time you see it, ask God to re-mind you of its significance. Boldly request God to sear your eyes with the light of eternity so that you can see your children as they truly are…invaluable and perfect creations of God.

2. Charles Haddon Spurgeon once said, "Carve your name on hearts, not on marble." Think of three people whose names are indelibly carved on the memory of your heart. What was it about them that left such an impression?

3. When the seasons of diapers, Little League, and driver's training have passed, when you are at last able to sit alone quietly for longer than two minutes at a time, when you are *there*…what do you want to have lived your life for?

Keeping Things Cool

Some Practical Strategies
for a More Peaceful Life

In the book of Ecclesiastes, we are told "there is an appointed time for everything. And there is a time for every event under heaven"—

A time to give birth and a time to die;
A time to plant and a time to uproot what is planted.
A time to kill and a time to heal;
A time to tear down and a time to build up.
A time to weep and a time to laugh;
A time to mourn and a time to dance.
A time to throw stones and a time to gather stones;
A time to embrace and a time to shun embracing.
A time to search and a time to give up as lost;
A time to keep and a time to throw away.
A time to tear apart and a time to sew together;
A time to be silent and a time to speak.
A time to love and a time to hate;
A time for war and a time for peace.

—Ecclesiastes 3:1-8

In the previous chapters, we've spent a lot of time examining the anger that we direct toward our children—and the painful fallout of that uncontrolled anger and rage. As we looked at "mantle realities," trigger points, and the difficult subject of discipline and abuse, perhaps you have been able to identify and "tear down" some of those "whys" in your own life—and to "weep" with the relief of knowing you are not the only mother who struggles with anger and rage. Perhaps you've "embraced" the truth of your past or "searched" for other reasons why anger has become such a powerful force in your life since you had children.

Now, at last, it's time to plant your feet firmly on the summit of your personal Mount Momma and declare, "I'm going to conquer this volcano—and this is how I'm going to do it!"

"How" is the focus of this chapter. It outlines a number of practical strategies that I hope will help equip you for taming Mount Momma in the days, weeks, and years to come.

I pray that at least one of the following strategies will be for you an idea whose time has come. May you "build up" your confidence and your parenting skills through the following words. May your home and your heart be filled with "laughing." May you learn new and effective strategies as you "shun embracing" the habits of your past and "give them up as lost." Most of all, may you find peace, joy, love, and contentment in your relationship with your precious children.

God bless you in your efforts to shape a more serene, more positive, and more godly home!

Strategy #1:
Stay in the Word

A few years ago, when Kristen and Ricky Neal were both under the age of four, I volunteered to host a women's Bible study in my home. I dusted every crevice of the house, swept under the sofa cushions, and prepared a tasty dessert for all the women to enjoy. I spent several hours preparing the lesson. By the morning of the study, I was ready, eager for 9:30 to arrive.

About 9:15 that morning, I took my two young children to a bedroom with a working VCR and instructed them to listen quietly to the 90-minute feature film, eat the Cheetos I had provided, and remain in the room.

That's right. I told my two small children to sit quietly by themselves for the next hour and a half!

The doorbell began ringing, and soon my living room was filled to capacity. I began our time together in prayer, asking God to bless His Word, bless the food, bless the women in attendance, bless the women who wanted to be there but couldn't, bless the...well, you get the picture. As I continued to request blessings for everyone in the free world, I heard my two children "wrestling"—that's mom-speak for fighting—in the upstairs hallway. Soon, the sounds of their battle overwhelmed my attempt at a proper invocation. I closed with a terse "Amen" and excused myself from the room.

They heard me coming up the stairs, so they fled to their assigned room. I found them lying on the bed, quietly watching the movie, with the bag of Chee-tos propped between them. I closed the door gently behind me and growled through gritted teeth, "What did Mommy tell you? I'm *trying* to have a Bible study downstairs, and I'm *trying* to teach ladies about Jesus! Now, *be quiet so Mommy can pray!*"

I then walked downstairs, sat in my favorite rocker, and began. "Okay, ladies, let's turn to our Scripture text, 1 Corinthians 13, and learn about the excellence of love."

Oh brother! In my zeal to perform something godly, I blew it big time! I had the right idea, attempting to put into practice the study of the Word in my life. However, there *are* a lot less stressful and child-friendly ways to pursue this goal than preaching about love to a houseful of women with your children confined out of the way behind closed doors.

Remember that basic reality we faced back at the beginning of this book—that having children changes everything? That includes your schedule, your energy level, your levels of concentration, and your needs and experiences. And it means that your approach to God's Word is probably going to have to change as well.

It's important not to place unrealistic expectations upon yourself in this area of Bible study. But it's even more important not to give up trying, because you *need* your time in the Word. You *need* to have your spirit lifted and your heart tuned and your mind renewed. You *need* God's point of view to balance and correct all the other messages your culture and your own expectations are giving you. You *need* to keep in mind why you're here and what you're supposed to be doing. And you *desperately need* God's peace and guidance if you are ever going to quell your Mount Momma tendencies.

So how can you manage to spend time in the Word without neglecting your duties as a mom or your own vital needs as God's child? To me, the key has been learning to do what you *can* right here, right now, without guilt.

This can be tough, especially if you had time before children when you could devote hours and hours to Bible memorization and study. For those of us who enjoyed cross-referencing and considered *Strong's Concordance* an invigorating read, scaling back study time to meet the demands of children can be a bit difficult. If you always tended to be a little lackadaisical about Scripture study in your pre-children days, you might find it even tougher to squeeze in *any* time with the Word.

No matter what your previous experience was, trust me, it really *is* possible to be both a busy mom and a woman of the Word. But you might need to be flexible in your expectations during the years when uninterrupted time simply doesn't exist. With that in mind, here are some practical ideas for building in some "Word Time" in the middle of your frantic, often frustrating days:

Real Mom Points to Practice

1. *Don't assume that the only worthwhile Bible study is a 60-minute-long study.* God honors our faithfulness as we grab the bits and pieces of the day and give them back to Him. Keep coming to Him in whatever way you can, and He *will* give you what you need. God commanded us to walk with Him; He wants us to become firmly rooted, built up, established, and overflowing in our faith and love for Christ. And He never, ever asks us to do something that He won't make possible.

2. *Take advantage of the multitude of free moments you encounter throughout your day to spend time in the Word.* Grab your Bible in the car and start reading as you wait at railroad crossings or in congested rush-hour traffic. You can also read as you wait through piano lessons, football practices, and dental appointments. As you wait for potatoes to cook or a baby to complete nursing…read, read, read, and read.

3. *Keep Bibles in convenient places.* You may not have set a definite time for reading the Bible or even thought about it. Instead of feeling guilty and just quitting altogether, try placing a Bible in a bathroom, near a kitchen table, next to the baby's bed, or in your car or van. Just

don't let your Bible fall into a damp tub or open-lidded toilet! Don't laugh—it's happened to me!

4. *Make use of special study Bibles, Scripture study guides, or lectionaries that help you devour Scripture in manageable "bites"*—carrying you through the entire Scripture over a year or two. These guides can help you get a sense of continuity in the Word and a feeling for how it all fits together without having to spend big chunks of time.

5. *Post favorite verses on your refrigerator and other often-viewed places.* Think of all the blank walls you look at as a mother—changing-table walls, kitchen walls, laundry room walls, and garage walls. Half of our lives as moms is spent looking at walls! So find a verse or two that really helps you, write it on an index card or sticky note, and start posting!

6. *Work at memorizing Scripture*—and include your kids in the memory work. My kids always liked this practice because, as kids, they learned the verses much faster. My competitive firstborn especially loved listening to me hem and haw long after she had the verse down pat.

7. *Experiment with other ways to make the Word part of your life.* Play recordings of the Psalms or musical settings of Scripture while you exercise or do dishes. Look for quality movies and videos that bring the Scriptures to life visually. Make up melodies for your favorite verses and sing them aloud—or sing well-known Scripture settings such as Karen Lafferty's "Seek Ye First the Kingdom of God."

TimeOut/Tamers: I have repeated 2 Timothy 2:13 over and over through the years whenever I felt like giving up the elusive goal of spiritual growth and Bible study. It's still a great source of strength to me, and I hope it will encourage you as well. "If we are faithless, He remains faithful, for He cannot deny Himself."

Strategy #2:
Make Space for Your Spirit

The demands upon a mother's time are limitless. That's just the truth. So unless we consciously *choose to create space* for our own spiritual needs, we will find ourselves suffocating beneath the weight of legitimate but overwhelming demands—or simply exploding out of anger and frustration.

I'm not talking just about Bible study here—though of course that's an absolutely critical part of it. I'm also talking about regularly making time for communion with the Lord and spiritual renewal. Just as your body demands food for energy, water for hydration, and sleep for renewal, so too your spirit—your soul—needs refreshment and nurturing. Never underestimate the power of a rested and renewed soul as you climb back to sanity!

You know all this, of course. So do I. But it's so easy to fall into the trap of seeing these spiritual disciplines as just another set of guilt-producing (and time-consuming) "shoulds." No wonder we tend to let them fall by the wayside! We need to keep reminding ourselves that spirit-building activities are lifelines, not obligations. You need them in order to be the kind of mother you want to be.

Here are a few ways you can lift your spirits and renew your soul—even in the middle of your busy, busy life with children.

Real Mom Points to Practice

1. *Carve out at least a few minutes a day for quiet time*—time when you can meditate on Scripture, pray, and just listen for God's still, small voice. Be gentle with yourself if

your quiet time lapses into nap time—God knows when you need sleep!—but keep on trying. When you are tempted to use your few quiet minutes to catch up on housework or other obligations, remind yourself that time with the Lord is even more important than a clean floor or a load of laundry.

2. *Be flexible about what time you do it.* Don't insist on waking up at 4:30 A.M. to have your quiet time just because someone told you 15 years ago that Jesus always did it that way. Jesus didn't have kids, and even if He had, He wouldn't have bitten their heads off five hours later in the day because He was sleep-deprived!

   If you truly feel called to an early-morning quiet time, that's great, but it's not the only way. Try nap times, just-after-bedtime times, right-after-everyone-leaves times, during-your-daily-walk times. Whenever you come to Him, God will be there!

3. *Make prayer a priority.* I don't know about you, but sometimes my brain refuses to wrap itself around the truth that the God of all creation longs to speak to us mothers. He does this through His written Word, but He also does it when we take the time to go to Him regularly in prayer—in both intentional "prayer times" and quickie "help me, Lord" prayers in the heat of the moment.

4. *Try the A.C.T.S. of prayer.* If you want to deepen your prayer life but don't know where to begin, you might find the acronym A.C.T.S. to be helpful. Begin with words of **A**cknowledgment, affirming that the Lord is worthy of praise and worshiping Him. Move from there to **C**onfession, admitting your sins to God and finding refreshment for your soul through His forgiveness. Continue with **T**hanksgiving, expressing appreciation

for the material and spiritual riches of your life. Then move into Supplication, making your wants, needs, and desires known to God. (Yes, He knows them before we speak, but again, something supernaturally refreshing comes as we trust Him with those things we need.)

5. *Begin a spiritual journal.* This is a great way to keep track of what God is doing even in the messy middle of your family life. I have written my journal in the pages and margins of my Bible. While there are a few longer entries, the majority consist of short phrases that summarize a concern, a need, or specific triumph—and a date. When I read back through my past margin notes, my spirit is refreshed as I recall God's faithfulness in the details of my life.

   For those who prefer to write in a notebook, I highly recommend Oswald Chamber's *My Utmost for His Highest* in journal form. Each day includes a timeless devotion and allows ample space for writing.

6. *Attend a conference or retreat.* These can be invaluable in helping you find nourishment for your soul—and a little time away from the kids can really help you keep your eyes on the kind of mother you want to be. Local churches often host one- and two-day retreats for a minimal charge during the fall and spring seasons.

   Nationwide conferences such as Women of Faith and Aspiring Women offer encouragement and fellowship for believers throughout the calendar year and are attended by thousands of participants. If babysitting is an issue, call a friend and offer to swap weekends off.

7. *Go on your own mini-retreat.* You really don't have to attend a big conference or travel a great distance for a time of spiritual refreshment. Quaint bed-and-breakfasts or even motels abound and can be quite reasonable for

an overnight stay. Or you could even cozy up for a morning or afternoon in a quiet restaurant or the lobby of a luxury hotel. Leave your preschoolers at Mother's Day Out. Bring your Bible, a hymnal, your journal, and perhaps a book you've been wanting to read. You'll come away from your "time apart" refreshed and renewed.

8. *Join together for support.* Christians were never meant to go it alone, though too often we try to do just that. You need to be in regular fellowship with other Christians— worshiping together in church, serving together in ministry, and getting to know each other on a deep level so that you can love and support one another.

This last level is one that a lot of Christians miss out on—it's just too easy to keep regular church activities on a small-talk level. So look for (or start!) a small prayer-and-share group in which you all aim at getting to know each other more deeply, sharing concerns, and praying together. Even an e-mail circle among like-minded Christians can be a lifeline.

9. *Read for guidance, encouragement, and inspiration.* Ask your local bookstore clerk, or search an online bookstore for books and magazines that inspire you and help you grow. During these "busy mom" years, however, it might be wise to think "short." Enjoy excerpts from Christian classics, short magazine articles, even lovely poems.

As your children grow a little more independent, consider joining or forming a book discussion group either in person or on the Internet. You can renew your thinking as well as your soul as you participate in lively conversations with fellow book lovers.

10. *When you can't read, listen.* Even when you have your hands busy with dishes or other activities, you can listen to recorded Scripture, tapes of Christian teaching, and to Christian programming available on broadcast radio and even on the Internet.

With the right downloads to your computer and the right audio accessories, you can listen to streaming Christian radio whenever you want. Grab your keyboard, go to <gospelcom.net>, click "Browse by Services" and go to "Live Online Radio." At this same website you can access more than 100 individual ministry web pages, many of which offer archived radio programs online.

Strategy #3:
Take Care of Your Physical Self

You're going to hate me for writing this...that's why I saved it for the last chapter of this book. Here goes: When I'm overweight (which is every other year), I tend to be a *very* crabby and cantankerous mother. When I am closer to my ideal weight, I feel better physically and also feel better about myself...and in my case at least, this translates into better, less volatile mothering.

After a routine exam three years ago, my doctor told me (no hinting around for this doc!) that I needed to lose at least 50 pounds. Fifty pounds? *At least?* As I drove home with Kristen—who has, enviably, inherited my husband's tall and slim DNA strand—I suddenly realized I needed to lose nearly the equivalent in weight of a ten-year-old child! Let's talk depressing!

I did lose the weight, though I've gained back 15 pounds over the course of a winter spent typing, typing, typing, and drinking a steady diet of caffeine-laden Pepsi. Despite this minor setback, I know that those pounds will have to come off somehow, because I'm just a happier camper when I weigh less and when the entirely new winter wardrobe I purchased last January still fits.

Now, please understand. I am not saying *a certain* weight is the ideal or that overweight people are bad mothers! I am saying that for some of us, for a variety of reasons, our propensity to "blow it" in anger is directly related to our physical condition.

And weight isn't the only issue, of course. Many of us mothers fail to take care of ourselves physically—and this failure can have a direct result on the way we parent our children. If you're like me, for instance, you get to the doctor maybe once a year. (You are so busy running your children to this clinic and that clinic that you seldom take the time to book *yourself* a 20-minute appointment.) You don't always eat the way you should or remember to take your vitamins—and yes, you *know* you should get more exercise, but who has time? Perhaps you've even gotten into the habit of overlooking physical and mental symptoms that are screaming for attention. To make matters even more complicated, you might be experiencing hormonal changes such as premenstrual syndrome or postnatal depression that can profoundly affect the way you relate to your kids.

Why is all this a problem when it comes to Mount Momma? Simply this: Being a mother is a physically demanding job, and any problem that affects our bodies will probably have an effect on how we relate to our children. When we are tired or run-down, when our hormones are out of whack, when we are in pain, when we are annoyed by nagging health concerns or ashamed of the state of our bodies, we also are likely to be irritable, short-tempered, and distracted. And then the chances of our blowing it in anger toward our children are that much greater.

Like it or not—and I don't always like it!—good physical condition (or lack thereof!) does play a crucial part in our climb to sanity. And while I am no expert, here are a few suggestions to get you started. If you already enjoy and practice a healthy lifestyle...then pray for the other millions and me!

Real Mom Points to Practice

1. *First of all, make an appointment with your doctor for a checkup.* Do it now! Bite the bullet, line up a sitter if you

need to, and go. Before you go, write down a list of physical issues or questions that may be nagging at you. If your doctor doesn't have time to talk about the things that are going on in your life or to consider any medical facts that may be contributing to your frustration and anger, then you have two choices: a) make another appointment just to talk or b) find another doctor.

2. *Do something*—anything—*about exercise.* There must be millions of other mothers who, like me, lived through the era of "feel the burn" and still cringe at the thought of sweating! But the sad fact is that exercise seems to be an important answer to both weight control and stress management, not to mention plain old good health.

   What you do is up to you and your doctor—the important thing is to do *something*, and to do it regularly. Try a brisk daily walk, a ten-minute stair-climbing session, an exercise video you can do with your kids—or just put your favorite CD on and dance!

3. *Focus on developing at least one good health habit.* Don't you sometimes feel overwhelmed by all the changes you think you'd need to make in order to "get in shape" or "change your eating habits"? You can overcome that feeling by choosing *one* good health habit you'd like to develop and working on just that one—taking a vitamin every day, drinking enough water, taking a walk every morning. Put your other desired changes on hold until you've mastered that one.

4. *Find some support.* For most of us, the journey to better health is a lot easier if we don't try to go it alone. Ask a buddy to be your "getting healthy" partner. Or take advantage of the resources that are available to support

you in your quest for better health—from Weight Watchers to recreation centers, from sports teams to support groups.

5. *Don't overlook your children as sources of support.* If you have the right attitude, their energy can be a real inspiration. Go for walks together. Do jumping jacks. Play kickball. Dance. Then enjoy a healthy picnic together. It's a lot more fun than doing it alone!

6. *Pay attention to your hormones.* If you are regularly bothered by nervousness and irritability, depression, emotional instability, difficulty concentrating, headaches, tender breasts, bloating, constipation, puffy ankles, acne breakouts, or just a sense that you're not yourself, be sure to ask your doctor about these symptoms.

   Depending on your stage of life, you may be suffering from premenstrual syndrome, perimenopause ("premenopause"), postnatal depression, or a hormonal imbalance. You may benefit from prescribed medicines such as diuretics, pain medications, tranquilizers or sedatives to relieve tension, or dietary supplements.

7. *Don't forget that mental health and physical health are closely connected!* If you are really struggling with an ongoing problem of anger and irritation toward your children, consider that you might be dealing with clinical depression or some other form of mental or emotional disorder. This doesn't mean you're crazy. It certainly doesn't mean that you have failed as a mother or a Christian—any more than does having diabetes or a sinus infection. However, it *does* mean you may need medication or counseling in order to get better. Appendix A suggests some symptoms to look for and some ways to find help.

8. *Don't forget to pray for the healing of any physical or mental problems that might be affecting your ability to be the kind of mother you want to be.* Above all, lean on your heavenly Father's tenderness and care. Yes, it's important to do what you can to take care of yourself—but you don't have to be a perfectly healthy specimen to be a good mom.

9. *Pamper your body when you can*—you'll be surprised at the emotional and spiritual benefits. Trade back rubs or foot rubs with your spouse or a friend. Or splurge a little at your favorite bath and body shop and reward yourself with a long, hot, soothing bubble bath after the kids are asleep. Light a candle or two, turn off the lights and relax…mmmm, I think I'll wind this up and go practice this point myself!

TimeOut/Tamers: If PMS is a problem for you, you can alleviate some of the discomfort by simply decreasing your salt intake. My ankles, which at times have resembled those of Babar the Elephant, have benefited from my using less salt during this time. Dieticians recommend eating a low-fat, high-complex carbohydrate diet and eating more frequent yet smaller meals. (Grazing at Sizzler twice daily doesn't count.) Also helpful—though very difficult for me to follow!—is to limit one's intake of caffeine.

Strategy #4:
Make Peace with Your Past

Let's face it: Some mothers reading this book have valid reasons for being angry and explosive!

Far too many of you experienced crushing blows of physical abuse, emotional abuse, and even sexual abuse as innocent young children. Far too many of you have struggled silently with that truth and have watched yourself teetering on the edge of abusive behavior towards your children.

Even if you were not actually abused as a child, there's still a chance that past experiences—death or divorce in the family, a severe financial reversal, a severe illness, or just poor parenting role models—are dragging down your relationship with your children. If you really want to move forward and get a handle on your anger problem, you're going to have to confront some of these past issues.

You're not alone—and the past doesn't have to control you. It's true that digging into the past can be painful and traumatic. But there are resources that can help you lay the past to rest and boldly embrace a future filled with joy and peace within your heart and home.

As I mentioned before, I have had to face this issue in my own life. Even if I wasn't physically harmed from birth to age three, I have learned enough about my family's problems to know that I must have witnessed abusive moments and probably did not walk away unscathed.

Another mother I spoke with has this to say about her own experience with physical abuse (and it can apply to many other circumstances, too): "When abused as children, we feel, and we are, powerless. We're not old enough or powerful enough to know how to stop it. But now, we have information all around us for the taking on how we can heal from this. We have adult minds capable of under-standing what could not be understood then. We have the choice to reach out for needed help: to surround ourselves with supportive others, so we're no longer alone in this."

A dear friend of mine was repeatedly molested by her adoptive father from age 7 until she was 13, at which age she began to protest and talk about his abuse to other members of the family. Now in her late 30s, she has just completed six years of Christian counseling, working hard with her counselor to defuse the power of her horrific past.

Before she began counseling, this friend would often call me, sobbing hysterically and trying to figure out why she felt so unattached to her children. I didn't have anything to tell her; I simply listened and prayed for her by long-distance phone. To release her, I knew that it would take God and the ministry of those He had gifted to deal appropriately with this issue in her life.

I just spoke with her three nights ago. Both of her sons are seeing a Christian counselor, and she was overjoyed to report to me that she's no longer afraid to be attached to her children. "I know most people won't understand what that means, " she laughed, "but I have found peace at last, Julie! I don't worry about abandoning them anymore. I understand the wound from which that emotion stemmed, and God has truly closed it—for the first time in 12 years I feel like I truly know what it means to love my children!"

Tears ran down my face as I listened to this dear friend speak about the burden that had been lifted through the wisdom of counselors and the mercy of our Lord and Savior Jesus Christ.

There *is* light at the end of the tunnel for you who feel your past has irretrievably tainted your mothering future. This light is held out to you by the Light of the world, Jesus Christ. He uses those who are faithful to the gifts and knowledge with which He has endowed them to be beacons of hope and change for those of you who struggle with the pain of yesterday. As you seek help and suggestions for dealing with your own painful past, hold on to this unshakable truth: " 'I know the plans that I have for you,' declares the LORD, 'plans for welfare and not for calamity to give you a future and a hope' " (Jeremiah 29:11).

Our God is the God of second chances. May the light of His love flood your being as your past is defused and your future is ignited for the glory of God!

Real Mom Points to Practice

1. *Face the fact that the anger you feel toward your children may really be coming from past issues.* Janice, an adult survivor of sexual abuse, puts it this way: "When you are abused as a small child, you aren't emotionally able or allowed to deal with the anger, so you bury it. Even from yourself. But the terrible thing about anger is that it always shows itself in some form or another.

   "The greatest thing I think you can do to help yourself is to identify your anger in its many forms. I have seen victims realize for the first time in their lives that something in their lives is actually anger! When you can connect the *why* you do something to the *what happened* in your past, you are able to release the anger."

2. *Don't carry your burden alone any more!* Tell your story—that you were abused as a child—to someone you love who is absolutely trustworthy. If you feel it's necessary, take this first step anonymously through telephone contact with a reputable counseling resource.

3. *Use a journal to tell yourself the story of your life.* Begin with your earliest memories, write out what comes to mind

next, and go from there. The point here is not to dwell on the past, but to increase your self-understanding and per-haps uncover hidden issues that might be influencing your present-day anger.

4. *Try to make forgiveness part of your healing process.* Ultimately, your freedom from anger over your past will be keyed to your ability to forgive those who have hurt you and perhaps forgive yourself for letting it happen. But true forgiveness usually takes time—you might not be able to go that far right away. It's all right to begin by simply being *willing* to learn to forgive someday and trusting God to take you to that point eventually.

5. *Beware of false forgiveness.* Sometimes what we call forgiveness is simply glossing over the past and pretending it wasn't important. You won't be able to solve your anger problems unless you choose to be honest with yourself!

6. *Use the help that's there.* There are numerous resources available for mothers dealing with past abuse and other traumas. These include and certainly aren't limited to intensive workshops for adult survivors of abuse, alcohol/drug treatment centers, workshops for survivors and their families, and trained counselors who assist survivors of physical abuse.

Most survivors of abuse or other childhood traumas will need some type of professional help in order to defuse this painful issue. Make an appointment with a counseling service of your choice to discuss your past and how you were parented. Seek professional counsel as you begin dealing with the ramifications of your childhood experience upon your parenting of your children.

7. *If your counselor tells you that nothing is wrong, yet your symptoms persist or you continue to have a nagging sense that something just isn't right, find another counselor.* You'll probably feel like you're doing something wrong, but be assured you are not. Taking charge of your own life and facing your past is a sure sign of maturity, so pat yourself on the back and keep at it until you have an answer.

   If money is a concern, acquaint yourself with the Red Cross and see if they offer any free or minimum-fee workshops on this subject. Don't be afraid to speak with the staff and let them know of your need for counseling and your budget requirements. Counseling services with sliding-scale fees are often available through county health services and clinics. It never hurts to ask! After all, these services are provided for your benefit.

8. *Don't forget to call on the Christian community for help.* Many churches have trained counselors who can deal with issues of family and parenting. If they are unable to meet your counseling needs, they should be able to refer you to someone who can. In addition, be sure to ask for prayer from your Christian brothers and sisters. If you are uncomfortable sharing exactly what happened, you can still ask for prayer about "difficult issues."

9. *Try a parenting class.* Age-specific parenting classes can be helpful resources for breaking the abuse cycle. I would certainly have benefited from a parenting class when my two oldest children were three and five. I didn't look for one because I thought it would scream, "You can't raise your kids right!" Instead I screamed at my kids. But I learned my lesson. When Patrick Michael

was small, I was actively involved in a parenting group. I wasn't afraid to admit, "I don't know what to do." We really don't have to go it alone any longer. Seize these resources and begin the process of defusing the power of your past.

Strategy #5:
Learn Anger Management Skills

Regardless of its origins, uncontrolled—and thus unhealthy—anger really can destroy your family. That's why it is so critical to put into practice sound and practical techniques to gain the upper hand over this emotion when it strikes.

Read over each suggested strategy and begin applying one technique on the day you read this material. These are just a few of the almost limitless helpful suggestions that are available online and in anger management workbooks.

You can begin to conquer poor anger management. You can find many resources through your local library, through Internet sites, and in a plethora of books dealing specifically with this subject matter. You may not be able to teach an old dog new tricks, but old and young mothers alike can learn new techniques for handling anger!

Real Mom Points to Practice

1. *Remember that feeling angry isn't "wrong."* Expressing that anger in unproductive and hurtful ways is!

2. *Change demands into desires.* Accept—really accept—the fact that you're going to have to give. You can't have everything your way.

3. *Learn to defuse your angry energy through relaxation.* Learn to relax by using deep-breathing techniques and picturing pleasant thoughts.

4. *Work off the excess energy.* Strenuous activity and exercise is an excellent tool for ridding yourself of pent-up tension and energy that could be released as anger toward your kids.

5. *Talk yourself through your anger.* Often it's the running dialogue that goes on in our heads that fuels the anger we feel. But you can turn the table by learning to "talk yourself through" your anger. Remind yourself that your children really aren't out to ruin your life! Stress to yourself that they really don't "always" do what they're doing. State the facts—"I'm having a miserable day—but getting angry will just make things worse!" Doing this will enable you keep a more balanced perspective on your situation.

6. *"Use your words"—positively.* Learn to express your attitudes, expectations, desires, and even your angry feelings directly and verbally instead of blowing up in frustration or expecting others to read your mind. As one writer put it, "Being assertive doesn't mean being pushy or demanding. It means being respectful of yourself and others."[1]

7. *Learn to express your feelings without assigning blame.* This will not only make a difference in your own mind; it will help keep the situation from escalating. One of the best ways to practice this is to use "I" messages in place of "you" messages: "I'm feeling very angry about this" instead of "You really make me mad."

8. *Go slow and soft.* While in a heated conversation (or while speaking to your child), slow down your speaking (literally) and soften your voice. It's difficult to explode when you're speaking in soft, restrained tones.

9. *Lighten up and laugh!* Sometimes we'd rather roll over and die before admitting to the humor of a stressful situation! But the book of Proverbs is right: Laughter has a strong medicinal effect, and studies show that

women who laugh a lot live longer than those who don't.

10. *Back off on the sarcasm.* Don't forget that sarcastic and hurtful "humor" can be simply a passive-aggressive form of anger!

11. *Journal your emotions of anger.* This is something you can teach your children also! Get your "angries" out...on paper. Consider your journal a safe, no-holds-barred place to vent—as well as a place to brainstorm creative solutions to anger-producing circumstances!

12. *Think ahead about anger-producing situations.* Prepare yourself mentally for circumstances that tend to push your buttons—and plan some strategies for defusing these situations. If certain relatives trigger your anger during the holidays or during visits, think ahead about the things you will do to avoid an angry confrontation—such as limiting the length of your visit or avoiding certain topics of conversation.

13. *In calm moments, focus on creative problem solving.* Strategize about ways you could rearrange your life to avoid circumstances that tick you off. For instance, if combing out your daughter's hair is a constant source of tension, give her the choice of learning to do her own hair or getting a cute short haircut!

14. *Don't overlook the possible need for help with anger issues.* A counselor with expertise in anger management can help. So can enrolling in a seminar or workshop on assertiveness training. (As hard as it may be to believe, a *lack* of effective assertiveness may be your problem when expressing your emotions.)

15. *Establish and teach your children clear guidelines for expressing anger.* If we insist "Don't look at me that way," "Don't stomp off like that," or "Don't speak to

me in that tone of voice," we are teaching them to suppress and avoid angry feelings. Instead, give your children boundaries in which they may express their anger (and it's often justified!) toward you, their siblings, or life in general.

Encourage them to express their frustration without using the word "you"—"Stop bugging me!" rather than "You bug me!" or "Leave me alone, that makes me angry," rather than "You always make me so mad!"

Teach them to talk themselves through times of anger. "I can control my anger," is something a young elementary student can begin repeating when angry. Children need to be taught that while it's okay to feel angry, it is unacceptable to hurt others in that anger.

Teach them to stuff their hands in their pockets or coat if they feel themselves curling up their fists and wanting to hit someone. And never forget they will do as we do, so practice what you teach!

16. *Don't forget to give* yourself *an occasional time-out!* Remind yourself of favorite ones mentioned in this book and invent your own, quick time-outs for moments of stress. Sometimes the best response to emotional situations is just to count to ten and wait things out.

17. *Never forget we do all things through Christ, who strengthens us!* That includes managing our anger.

Strategy #6:
Have a Plan for Discipline

Here's a slogan to post on your mirror, your refrigerator, and every door of your house: When it comes to parenting, only chickens should wing it!

That's been a hard lesson for me personally because I've always had a gift for flying by the seat of my pants. I've pulled myself out of many a jam sheerly through the skill of verbal two-stepping. It isn't unusual for me to entertain captive audiences in elevators or grocery lines using my rapier wit alone. (Okay, I am often the only one truly entertained by the rapier wit, but I sure do like using it—especially in front of an audience.)

Winging it, in fact, has always been a pretty successful strategy for me...until three babies permanently grounded me. Yes, the fact that my payload was much heavier after children may have accounted for some of my problem, but the true issue was that the best parenting requires a plan. A little advance preparation can do a lot to reduce stress in both parent and child—and that in turn can cut down significantly on the size and number of Mount Momma eruptions in a household.

I should have learned this long ago, of course. Professor Emmett Wade pounded it into my head over and over during my sophomore year of college. In his distinctive Southern drawl he would say, "Ah...[he always started with "Ah"], you would be wise to remember the following, Miss Patrick [me before marriage]: Failing to plan is planning to fail." This little pronouncement usually came while he was handing me back a research paper completed three hours before its due date, marked C-minus.

If you're going to do any job well, you'd better have a plan. And that's especially true of parenting—no matter how good you are at improvisation. If you try to wing it with your kids, you're begging for a C-minus in mother-hood! More to the point, you'll be a lot more likely to blow it in anger.

With that in mind, let's consider some invaluable practical strategies of discipline and parenting that can lighten the load tremendously if followed. (For detailed help in this area, I wholeheartedly recommend Kevin Leman's book *Making Children Mind Without Losing Yours!* His suggestions make sense, are doable, and believe it or not, they work!)

Real Mom Points to Practice

1. *Try to anticipate misbehavior and establish consequences ahead of time.* Though your kids will occasionally surprise you, it's not really that hard to imagine what your children are likely to do. They will sometimes disobey (or misunderstand) your instructions. Things will be broken. Words will be spoken. Think ahead and anticipate what your response will be. Aim to have as few impromptu rules as possible.

2. *Be sure to follow through with the consequences you have established.* Children have the uncanny ability to jump on a missed consequence like flies to honey, and letting down your guard will make it twice as difficult to return to a place of control. If you said it would happen, make sure it happens.

3. *Avoid setting yourself and your children up for failure.* Consider your child's temperament, her energy level (has she missed a nap?), the activities you plan to do, and the worst-case scenario for any particular planned activity. Sometimes simply postponing a trip to the

grocery store when your toddler is tired and cranky can cut out the need for any discipline at all.

4. *Don't make consequences so long or harsh that they lose their meaning.* Keep pulling your focus back to "What do I want to accomplish?" Aim at improving your child's future behavior, not exacting punishment for mistakes.

5. *Involve the entire family, especially your spouse or other care-givers, in determining a family policy regarding discipline.* Will you use time-outs? Natural consequences? Corporal punishment? What forms of punishment will be off limits: name calling? spankings with an object rather than a hand? other family members disciplining your child? If possible, write down what you determine on a chart for everyone's reference.

6. *Have your child tell* you *what the rules of the house are.* You may well discover he doesn't know everything you think he does—or that something that seems obvious to you is mystifying to her. Clarify your expectations before you hold your children responsible for meeting them.

Strategy #7:
Honor Your Child's Bent

Charles Swindoll, an author I highly respect and appreciate, once penned the following in a book titled *The Strong Family:*

> Do not think that just because you have conceived, carried and finally given birth to your little one, you automatically know your child. Nor can you say you know him or her just because you live in the same house. I must say, categorically, you do not. Knowing your child takes time, careful observation, diligent study, prayer, concentration, help from above, and yes, wisdom. The two essentials are desire and time. If you really want to know, and if you're willing to invest the time, God will honor your efforts. He will enable you to know your child.[2]

I first read this passage on an afternoon in 1992 when I was on "toddler furlough," a rare afternoon alone. I had slipped into my favorite place for shopping *without* little ones—the local bookstore. At the time I was wallowing in the muck over feelings of anger toward Kristen and Ricky Neal. It seemed I had two emotions when dealing with their childish antics, joy or rage, and once again I was searching for a book that might offer hope for a horrible mom like me.

Swindoll's book looked promising, so I took it home, and at the end of a long, draining day I read the section entitled "Your Baby Has the Bents!" In a few brief paragraphs I discovered a fresh perspective that would change my parenting life. I highlighted and drew exclamation points all around the page where Swindoll skillfully dissects Proverbs

22:6: "Train up a child in the way he should go, even when he is old he will not depart from it."

I had read that Scripture before, of course. Millions of parents, for countless generations have recited, claimed as their own, and clung to this Scripture. But Swindoll gave me a whole new perspective on it that day:

> The verse is not just referring to the ultimate goal of bringing a child into right relationship with God and ultimately into a happy and prosperous future. It refers to the makeup of a child—his unique characteristics and mannerisms, which Scripture calls, "his way." The Hebrew word is *dereck*. There is no precise book for raising children. Hence, Solomon writes, "Train up a child in keeping with or accordance to his mannerisms, his characteristics, his way." Wise are the parents who believe that and adapt their training accordingly.[3]

Is that refreshing or what? Our children have a natural "bent," a way about them that comes…well, naturally! This includes what some call personality and others define as temperament. It also includes such qualities as physical energy level.

You Can Start Learning Now

If you've never read or studied about temperaments, *this* is the time to begin. Your child has a natural, God-given "bent," and a wise mother—that's you and I—will study and learn the direction that "bent" leans and focus on helping the child become who he or she was meant to be. A foolish mother disregards this biblical and behavioral truth and suffers the consequences.

For example: I well remember a time several years ago when my second-born child threw a complete fit in the middle of our local Sears store. Not surprisingly, his tantrum precipitated my own fit of anger. I power-walked to the parking lot with said child bringing up the rear and shouting, "No, Mommy! Please no, no, no…" over and over again. Really loud.

Looking back, though, I can see the mistakes I made in light of his "bent." One was taking an active, curious, self-confident child into a hardware department and *expecting* him to stay off the bright red lawnmowers with lots and lots of gadgets. (After all, his *father* can't!) My second big mistake was going to the shopping mall during naptime. Ricky Neal was always a "Same Bat-time! Same Bat-station!" type of kid. He was a schedule lover and could not tolerate missing this important part of the day.

Now, that's not earth-shatteringly complex. I could have saved myself a lot of frustration and heartache if I would simply have taken the time to consider my son's "bent" before I took off on certain excursions.

The more I've studied temperaments, "bents," and God-given tendencies, the more I've come to love all the different people in my life. Just as I am what I am (spontaneous, opinionated, bombastic, and a lover of fun), so too are my mother, father, relatives, and treasured friends, each with his or her own tendencies and leanings. This has nothing to do with one person's being more worthy of kindness or love because of particular personality traits. It *is* about unconditional love…and that is difficult in the best of situations. But I've found that understanding and accepting the many ways human beings can differ helps make loving them easier.

Even more important, understanding and accepting the characteristics that make each of our children unique can help us establish a more loving, more patient, and considerably less angry home.

Real Mom Points to Practice

1. *Think back on some of your Mount Momma eruptions.* Try to remember two specific times when your child acted absolutely like a maniac or acted in a manner that sent you into a full-blown explosion. Now, reevaluate that moment in light of that child's God-given "bent"— natural mannerisms, characteristics, and ways. Write down some things you could have done differently to avoid that moment of mothering madness.

2. *For every "bent" of your child that you consider a weakness, make yourself say aloud how it can be a strength.* Examples: "Strong-willed" can be "tenacious," "oversensitive" becomes "compassionate." Train yourself to speak about the strength, not the weakness.

3. *Spend a little time researching temperaments.* It's not only fun and fascinating, but it can really open your eyes to what you can change about your children and what you can't. Appendix B contains some helpful references and resources to help in your search.

4. *Honor your child's stage of development as well as his or her "bent."* While it's true that every child is unique, it's also true that most children go through predictable stages of development. No matter how hard you push, you can't force children to be ready for potty training, recognizing ABCs, or managing fine motor skills—and growing angry over their failures in this regard won't help anyone.

   You can save yourself and your children a lot of grief if you learn to adjust your expectations to each child's developmental level. See Appendix C for a summary of what you can expect from children at certain ages—but even then, keep in mind that different children mature at different rates.

5. *Keep in mind that the Golden Rule applies to your children, too.* You would like to be accepted and loved for who you are. Pray to God for the ability to do the same with your beloved children.

Strategy #8:
Learn to Discern

One of the most important steps in climbing back to the summit of sanity is learning to discern and evaluate the beliefs or teachings that we come across in the books, magazines, and television in our day-to-day lives.

There are two things we need to think about here. First, what we watch, listen to, and read *does* influence the way we live—whether we are conscious of the influence or not. Second, and more important, we actually do *choose* the ideas and images we let into our lives.

Here's an example. Several months ago, my friend Margie and I were discussing what I was writing. She told me that, after listening to my argument that society clearly articulates a "children are burdens" mentality through the media, she began seeing some things for the first time—or, better said, she began to think more about what she saw or heard.

"I got to thinking about the television show *The Brady Bunch*," she said. "Everyone vilifies it now, but what was so bad about it?" She went on to note, "It's as if it's a bad thing when a television program portrays a family as functional and loving."

Exactly! That's just what I mean about discerning. So often the messages that our society feeds us about families, children, and parents is faulty at best and dangerous at worst. And because these messages are all around us, it's easy to subconsciously buy into them—even ideas and attitudes we don't really believe.

Since we're already talking TV, let's take a look at what we view and apply a discerning eye to its positive or negative effect upon our mothering.

First, who is your favorite television mom? Go ahead, say it out loud. No one's going to pay any attention to a mother talking to herself—it happens all the time!

Now, why is this particular mom your favorite? Does she make you laugh? Does she have character strengths you admire? What qualities does she represent as a mom?

I'll tell you my personal favorite in the year 2000: Debra Barone on the CBS show *Everybody Loves Raymond*. This spunky character is played by actress Patricia Heaton, a real-life mother of three children who has juggled real-life morning sickness, postpartum depression, and lactation soreness, all while performing for a camera. That's what makes her so appealing to me.

In a 1998 interview with the *Minneapolis Star-Tribune*, Patricia Heaton acknowledged the universal chord that her character strikes with her female audience:

> I feel privileged to be able to portray realistically a mother on TV. I just think it's nice as a mother in my own life to be able to have that opportunity on TV to have her be real and funny and crazy a little bit. I found in being a mother that it's a really hard, important job, and I think it kind of gets short shrift on TV...The wives and the moms on most family shows are the most underwritten, under-appreciated roles, and the hardest to do.[4]

I identify with Debra because I too am married to a Raymond—a sweet and endearing man with a few real-life annoying tendencies that become especially pronounced around the sixteenth of each month! I feel Debra's pain as she deals with three children, a husband, and loving but intrusive in-laws, and once a week I can laugh out loud and scream, "Oh my gosh! That is you exactly!" to my sheepishly smiling husband. I know it sounds wacky, but a pretend woman named Debra Barone has helped me view my husband's idiosyncrasies with a smile and chuckle. I consider her influence quite positive indeed.

But what about soap operas? I haven't watched a daytime drama since 1984, but I'll still bet that no one on those shows ever goes to the bathroom except for a luxurious bubble bath with a hunky man and 492 lit candles. I'll bet a woman who just experienced an emergency C-section still looks like Cindy Crawford on the cover of *Vanity Fair,* and I'll bet most of the people she knows are involved in unspeakably painful experiences that generally have to do with hopping from bed to bed, throwing away marriages, and cheating on the ones they have. Life in Soapland is pretty predictable. Obsession, lust, and betrayal are usually the set menu for each day. The same is true for some of those nighttime dramas and a lot of romance novels.

In light of these musings, think about what you watch most often, as well as what you read and listen to and surf through online. Consider how it might affect your opinion of marriage—your opinion of your children—your opinion of the hunky man next door. Seriously, *are* the covenants of marriage honored? Are marital bonds kept in the books and programs you "veg" out on? Do the books you read *strengthen* your commitment to your children and *nurture* your emotions towards them, or do the characters and settings play to your own fantasies of singleness and no responsibilities?

A few years ago I actually had to quit reading a certain book series—*not* because of risqué material, but because the male characters in it were *too* virile, *too* strong, and *too* gifted in carpentry skills! After reading each book I would look at my husband and think, "I'll bet he couldn't build a sod house, save the ranch from a forest fire, or build me a romantic outhouse like that amazing man did!" Rick was being forced to compete with a male lead who didn't even exist! And please understand—there was nothing really wrong with those books! The problem was the negative influence they were having on my heart.

More Important Areas for Good Judgment

Obviously, TV and books are just two examples of the massive pop culture that surrounds us and influences us. Music is another biggie, especially if you have teens and pre-teens in the house. Remember how powerful the songs were that you listened to when you were their age? I used to lie on my bed listening to Barry Manilow sing "Mandi," and weeping like a baby—and that was *after* I knew that Mandi was a dog!

Music seems to have the uncanny ability to reach deep inside us—and the fact that we listen to songs we like over and over gives it even more power. But with music, too—especially lyrics—we need to stop and think: What is the overall message I'm taking in? Since so many songs seem to be about relationships, it's not a bad idea to consider what they are implying. That love can never last? That feeling good is the only thing to look for? That sex is the logical outcome of any male-female relationship?

Yet another important area that calls for discernment is the "advice culture"—from talk shows like *The Oprah Winfrey Show* to the various Dr. Experts who pronounce wisdom on topics from sex to child-rearing. Now, I'm not saying that all these sources of influence are bad. Some are very good—but we need to pay attention to the real messages they are sending to us and to our children. Even our favorite Dr. Expert needs to be followed intelligently, not blindly. All this advice needs to be viewed through the lens of a discerning spirit.

This brings us to the very important subject of how we gain discernment. When I need wisdom to know what is best in books, television, and culture, I believe in going to the Word of God. I apply this verse from Philippians 4:8 to any questionable areas that demand a discerning look: "Finally, brethren, whatever is true, whatever is honorable, whatever is right, whatever is pure, whatever is lovely, whatever is of good repute, if there is any excellence and if anything worthy of praise, dwell on these things."

Real Mom Points to Practice

1. *Take a good hard look at your family's favorite television programming and see if it meets the test of Philippians 4:8.* Allow your children to be involved in this process. Take a sheet of paper and divide it into specific categories. Here are a few I chose when my family did this: cursing, taking God's name in vain, disobeying parents, making fun of God or those who believe in God, and goofy-acting fathers. (I chose the last one because at the time it seemed that every television father was either a half-wit or a jerk—not exactly how the Word of God portrays fathers.) We then watched our usual television programs, and every time we viewed one of the listed offenses, we put down a tally mark. Kristen was old enough to catch several sexual wrongs, and we noted those also. After two hours of "family" programming, we turned off the set and discussed our findings. We were all surprised at the high number of marks, particularly in the "disobeying parents" category. This exercise gave us a wonderful springboard for discussion—and our viewing habits changed.

2. *When you (or your children) play the radio, listen to the words.* Examine carefully the messages that are pounding their way into your brain along with the

catchy beat and bouncy melody. You may or may not choose to stop listening to certain stations, but at least you'll be aware of what you're listening to.

3. *Don't forget commercials and ads.* It's hard to avoid the influence of ads because they're loud, repetitive, and *everywhere.* But advertising can be especially deadly in feeding an attitude of discontent with ourselves and with our families. Try to get in the habit of talking back to commercials—especially with your children—examining what they're really implying about how much you need in order to be happy.

4. *Don't just think negative.* Make a point of seeking out books, movies, TV shows, and music that actually build up your family. Fill your heart and mind with positive images of what you want your life to be. For instance, I highly recommend the recorded collection of songs called *Sleep Sound in Jesus* by Michael Card, even if—especially if—you no longer have infants or toddlers. Mr. Card's beautiful words will beckon you to draw your children close and will remind you of their preciousness. I desperately need that reminder in the midst of dealing with two children going into puberty.

5. *Don't forget to pray for discernment* and search the Scriptures for answers to your questions about what is okay and what is best. God gave you your brain, and He will give you the resources you need to put it to work.

Strategy #9:
Learn to Let Go

It should have been a peaceful and joyous Sunday morning. Just the night before, while I was reading aloud to the children, Ricky Neal had announced in a solemn and serious tone, "Mom, I need to ask Jesus to come into my heart."

My heart quickened. I quickly finished the chapter I was reading, tucked Kristen into bed, and walked with my son back to his room. He sat on his *101 Dalmatians* comforter while I asked him a few simple but eternally important questions: "Why do you want to ask Jesus into your heart? What is sin? What sin do you need Jesus to forgive?"

I listened in awe as my six-year-old son prayed aloud, "Jesus, wash away my sin, because I don't want death or hell."

What joy! I had been granted the privilege of witnessing my son reborn as a son to God the Father. He had been reborn by the power of Jesus Christ's death and resurrection! We quickly phoned his father, who was working his evening shift, and Ricky told his daddy all about the decision he had just made. Then I tucked him in to bed, sharing with Ricky how excited our church family would be to hear of his decision. I also explained that his daddy and I would stand by him as he shared the good news with our small congregation the next morning.

At that point though, Ricky Neal was yawning. After all, he was six, and his bedtime had already passed. He couldn't have cared less about my spiel about the congregation.

Sunday morning arrived, and *I* was eager to share the news with our friends at church. Soon we were at Bushnell Baptist Church and found ourselves commencing routine in-church procedures: "Sit still," "Don't talk while we're praying," "Take your foot off the pew," and so on. It didn't take long for 14-month-old Patrick to begin fussing, so I rose to take him to the crying room. As I stepped into the aisle, I noticed Ricky Neal lying against his father. I snapped my fingers, indicating he should quit slouching and pay attention.

I followed about three words of the sermon while being held hostage in the crying room. As soon as the final hymn began, I scurried back to my seat, eager for what would come next. I eased back into place, and my gaze settled upon the sleeping figure of my six-year old son.

Annoyance began to creep over me—first, because I don't allow the kids to sleep during church, and second, because this was such an important morning.

I looked at my husband and whispered, "Why did you let him fall asleep? He needs to go to the front of church in about 30 seconds and let the others know what he did last night."

"He's not feeling well," Rick replied. "Let it go."

Let it go? No. I scooted over to Ricky Neal and gently jiggled his shoulder.

"Ricky, get up."

His eyelids flickered. He looked up at me for just a second. Then the eyelids closed again.

"Ricky Neal, you need to wake up!" I put my hands beneath his arms and pulled him upright. While the third and final verse was being sung, my son began to cry. His father mouthed the words again, "Let it go."

Well! I loosened my grip on Ricky Neal, glared at my husband, and began tapping my right foot (a key indicator that I'm getting ready to blow!).

The pastor ended the service with a benediction, and I stalked to the minivan with Patrick on my right hip and Kristen and Ricky Neal in my wake. As the children buckled up, my husband asked, "What's the matter, babe?"

"Nothing," I replied. (Tap, tap, tap, tap.)

Kristen—the intuitive child—chimed in, "She's mad at Ricky beca—"

I silenced her with a hard glare and spit out, "I'm—not—mad—at—Ricky Neal."

The lie sat bitterly upon my tongue as tension and toe-tapping filled the van.

Let it go.

We returned home, and Ricky Neal spent the remainder of the day asleep in bed. My toe-tapping had ceased as I was cooling his 103-degree fever with a cool washcloth. I felt worse than he did, if that was possible! I had allowed the joy of my son's salvation and the childlike wonder of that holy moment to be straitjacketed into a controlled procedure and form! I had succumbed yet again to the overwhelming need to control...everything!

Sin had won and Ricky Neal had lost that morning. While he slept and his body began to cool, I sat near his bedside, watching him breathe. Quietly I confessed, "I'm sorry, Ricky Neal. Your mom can be such a jerk sometimes!"

Let it go, Rick wisely counseled, *let it go.*

Trust God to Hold Things Together

It's a truth I just can't get through my head sometimes: Everything doesn't depend on me—and everything doesn't have to happen just the way I planned it. I could save myself a lot of frustration and anger if I could just get a better sense of what I really can control.

Is that a problem for you, too? Most of us could let go of two-thirds of what we think we have to control. The world would keep revolving. Our families would keep on functioning. As mothers, we keep a lot of plates spinning at one time, but how many of them could be gently laid aside if we'd only give up a little control?

I heard Annie Chapman speak on this subject about three years ago. She repeatedly said that for many of us it isn't the need to keep things going that causes us to lose our minds; it's the matter of trying to control everything while it's going. We mean well, we really do—but we have to learn to let it go.

Here's what we need to learn—sometimes over and over again. God is the one who's really in control. Always. He never sleeps. He never slumbers. He is never caught off guard. He is never surprised by a fever, and He isn't limited by baby mobile colors in developing a child's intellect. He knows what has happened, what is happening, and what will happen in each of our lives. Best of all, He is faithful, He is trustworthy, and *He* is in control of control!

The book of Colossians says it best: "He is before all things, and in Him all things hold together" (1:17).

If God holds things together, what that means is we *don't have to*. More important, we're not supposed to. When we try to be in charge of everything, we're really trying to take God's place. No wonder we grow frustrated and angry. We're just not up to the job of being God!

And so here's a new motto for mothers: *Let it go.* When your kindergartner insists on wearing a week-old nightshirt (that he adamantly proclaimed "don't smell!") to class...*let it go.* When your pre-teen son blames you for his genetic propensity to trip over his own feet and get hit by wild baseball pitches...*let it go.* When you feel it is your duty to control your children 100 percent of the time in public...*let it go!*

Let it go. Say those three words aloud a time or two. Get comfortable with the way in which they roll off your tongue. After that, the only thing you need to do is learn to take it seriously!

By now you may be protesting, "But I can't let *everything* go!" And that's true. As mothers, we are responsible for nurturing our children, teaching them, meeting their needs the best we can. To a certain extent we can control the environment where our children live—whether it's ordered or chaotic, dirty or clean. As long as we are bigger than they are, we can control to a certain amount where they go and what they do. But so often I think we fall into thinking we have to control almost everything that happens in our home. When we do that, we're just setting ourselves up for frustration, anger, and more Mount Momma eruptions.

This issue of what we can control and what we can't can really be a tricky one. In times of confusion, it might be helpful to focus on what God *does* want and expect us to control. Proverbs 25:28 sums it up precisely: "Like a city that is broken into and without walls is a man who has no control over his spirit."

In his commentary, Matthew Henry explains that brief Scripture this way: "Here the good character of a wise and virtuous man is implied. He has the rule of his own thoughts, his desires, his inclinations, his resentments, and keeps them all in good order."[5]

Change those pronouns to female, and you have specific—and challenging—instructions for a mom! More than once I've yelled at one of my kids, "You've got to learn to control yourself!" I would do well to follow my own advice! As mothers, our top priority must be the control of our own emotions. That's half the battle with this problem of anger and rage, because when we let ourselves come unhinged, it's all downhill from there.

The good news of course is that although God expects us to control ourselves, He also gives us the help we need to do just that. When God strengthens us, control issues are less likely to build into resentments and resentments into outward actions, and outward actions into regrettable words and deeds.

Here's an example of what I mean. One big control issue for me relates to my children's lack of enthusiasm for household chores. I want them to make their beds, fold the towels, and pick up trash in the front yard with a bit more...gumption. Instead, they sulk through the house and look as though at any time they may need CPR—and pretty soon I can feel my jaw beginning to clench. But the truth is that I can't really *make* my kids enjoy their chores. I don't really have any control over how they feel, and my control over how they act is really pretty limited. But I *can* control the way I approach the problem of chores. I can ask God to teach me the best manner in which to deal with grumpy kids and still get the jobs done in the process. I can control my own spirit...and trust God to take care of the rest.

TimeOut/Tamer: Reinhold Niebuhr's famous prayer as adapted by Alcoholics Anonymous is great for moms with control problems:

God, grant me the serenity to accept the things I cannot change;
Courage to change the things I can;
And the wisdom to know the difference.

Real Mom Points to Ponder

1. *Make a list of the issues that tend to keep you and your children at odds.* Write down as many issues you can think of. Then go back through and mark the three or four most important issues—the ones that really will affect the outcome of your child's life. The rest are probably items you can choose to let go.

2. *Choose one control issue you really struggle with.* Write that specific issue in the margin next to Proverbs 25:28 and date it. As of that moment you are going to begin

praying and ask God for His supernatural strength to help you rein in that issue as you seek to control your own spirit. Over the next few months, whenever you have a success in this area, add a checkmark in your Bible.

3. *Actually write down three areas where you are not going to "sweat it."* Hair? Makeup? Jeans in church? Friday-night bedtime?

4. *Ask someone you trust whether overcontrol is a problem for you.* Go to someone else for a second opinion. Listen to the answers you get.

5. *Build up your "trust muscles."* Often our controlling tendencies are really evidence of a lack of trust in God that He will take care of us and the people we love. When you pray, picture placing yourself and your family in God's large, capable hands. Meditate on that image in your mind. Thank God that, no matter how hard we try to control things, He's still the one in charge.

Strategy #10:
Childproof Your Mouth

Here's another control issue, one that is so important for many mothers—me, in particular—that it deserves its own section. James 1:26 sums it up beautifully: "If anyone thinks himself to be religious, and yet does not bridle his tongue but deceives his own heart, this man's religion is worthless."

If you're like me, prone to talk before you think, this Scripture is really a wake-up call. We can do so much damage to our children when we fail to control our tongues, especially in the heat of anger. And I think this verse speaks to more than just the words we say. I believe it speaks to the intonation, the inflection, and the timing of the words we speak.

I can say "I love you," for example, in a dozen ways, with varying cadence and emphasis on individual words.

There's "I love you" said wearily, as if I'm suffering for Jesus just to do it.

Or there's "I love you" spoken sharply, as if to say"...but barely."

"I love you" spoken firmly can imply "and that will never change."

James gives us the key instructions for control in this area: "Everyone must be quick to hear, slow to speak and slow to anger" (1:19). When you begin putting this verse into practice, you will stop listening just so you can hear a pause where you can jump in. You will take a breath and ask yourself, "Does this really need to be said?" *before* you speak. You will have fewer regrets over your words and will find that you regret saying and find you offend people less often in the heat of impassioned speech.

I'm not saying we all need to shut up and never speak our minds. But we do need to pray for control before we open our mouths. And we may well need to do some work on changing our habits of speech that include those ugly words—the ones that just slip out before we know what we've said. Just as we place toxic chemicals on shelves far from the reach of children, we need to shelve far away from us the toxic words, phrases, and comments that poison our speech.

Listed below are several suggestions I hope will help you in this area. Take your time. Determine what toxin needs to be dealt with first, and deal with it. Don't attempt to banish everything in one fell swoop. It took you years to develop your speech patterns, and it will probably take a significant amount of time to change them. Take it one day at a time, one toxic problem at a time, and you will find lasting change.

It can be done. Trust me. If I could learn to control myself and childproof my own toxic mouth, any mother can!

Real Mom Points to Ponder

1. *Turn on a tape recorder before breakfast or another meal and record the way you speak to your children.* The very act of doing this will make you more aware of what you say (or want to say)—and listening to the tape later might help you pinpoint some areas you need to work on.

2. *List some of the toxic words and phrases you want to eliminate from your speech with your children.* (Start with that simple, no-brainer phrase "You're stupid.") Write these words and phrases on a large sheet of paper. If you have a computer and printer, set the font size at sixteen

or eighteen and print them out. Now, post them somewhere where you will be reminded of their ugliness.
Read them aloud from time to time as a reminder of
what you *don't* want to say!

3. *Think ahead about how you are going to talk to your children
   when they push your buttons.* Don't let yourself be pulled
   into a toxic shouting match with a 3-year-old son or a
   12-year-old daughter. You will do one of two things:
   1) say something you regret; 2) say something you
   regret. Instead, rehearse some calm, positive responses
   that you could use in a stressful situation.

4. *Balance any verbal slips you might make by becoming your
   child's greatest cheerleader!* Beware of the tendency to
   complain about your children to others. Instead, let
   people hear you speak positively and proudly. Let your
   children hear you say—loudly and often—"I'm so glad
   I had you!"

Strategy #11:
Simplify, Simplify!

Someone once said, "We can do anything—but not everything."

Amen to that.

We live in a time of infinite, limitless opportunity. When astronauts routinely travel to space and back, most Americans don't even bother to watch the lift-off. Armed with a mouse and modem, you can point and click your way to Singapore and download 800-page e-books by famous authors. We are busy, busy, busy, but are we doing what's best and what's most joyous?

Most of us *know* we're too busy. We complain about it with one another or flop ourselves into bed at night with a vow to slow down. We worry that we just don't have enough time to spend together as a family. At the same time, most of us still find it difficult to establish boundaries and keep them...for the long haul.

We all need *significant* time for rest, renewal, and just enjoying life. We need unscheduled hours to just play, talk, or simply be—together or alone. Such a cushion of time can be a significant eruption preventer. But it can't happen unless we make it a priority, and that means learning to say no.

I'm not just talking about eliminating the frivolous or unimportant things in our lives. Most of us took care of that a long time ago. Now we are down to the toughest step, which involves choosing the best and saying no to the rest—and the rest is often quite good too.

Teaching Sunday school, participating in a book club, working out three times a week, and leading a children's musical may all be wonderful and enjoyable things to do with one's time. However, when you are tailoring yourself a revamped schedule that makes more space for rest and family time, something will probably have to go. This phrase can be the key to sanity: *Pick the best…say no to the rest.*

This was harder for me to do in the early years of marriage and mothering. I felt guilty if someone invited us over or asked Kristen or Ricky to come play at their house and I said no. Maybe it's because I'm older and more mature, but now I don't feel guilty saying no to just about anything. I've gone to cramming our weekends with company and out-of-town places to hanging out at the house and watching Rick play baseball in the yard with the kids. Our yard tends to be cluttered with friends' bicycles, and the refrigerator is routinely cleared of all "decent food," and every once in a while I'll have to shout, "Every kid not related to me by blood, back to their own home." Then Kristen, Ricky, Patrick, and I sit back for a mean game of Monopoly.

The point of it all, of course, is to simplify your life, to reduce your Mount Momma stresses, and to remember why you all liked each other in the first place. "Choose the best, say no to the rest" is really just another way of saying yes to a strong, friendly, *unexplosive* family life!

Here are just a few examples of how you can begin the process of simplifying. As you mull over the following suggestions, pick the easiest one and do that within the next eight hours. The goal is to curtail your times apart as a family and to create a new schedule where you are joining each other for joyous moments of family life.

Real Mom Points to Practice

1. *Start by taking out the easy stuff.* Sit down with your calendar and make a list of everything you do outside the home. About each one, ask yourself the following: "Do

I or does someone in our family truly enjoy this?" You might be surprised to find that some of the things you do, you simply don't enjoy. Unless they are absolutely necessary, why continue to do them? Cross them off your list first!

2. *Remind yourself of what is truly important.* Go back and reread your list (from the end of chapter 6) of what you think is important in the light of eternity. Now read through your calendar again and apply those truths to your activities and interests. Are they contributing or causing a distraction?

3. *Get a clear picture of which activities are truly "the best."* Working from your calendar, make a list of all the activities you and your children are involved in. Look at your list and underline the three activities that you feel are truly most important (not "most urgent" or "what I don't dare give up"). Which will make an eternal difference in your life and your children's lives? Which are most effective in helping them grow? Which can be done only by you and nobody else? Getting a sense of what you care about most will help you be strong when you set about eliminating other activities.

4. *Don't cut out every "just for me" activity.* Your goal is to make life more manageable and joyous for everyone, not to eliminate every activity that *you* enjoy in favor of activities for your children. It really is all right to keep a few things that refresh your spirit away from your family—to keep the nights out with your girlfriends or choir practice as one of the "best."

5. *Start cutting—one activity at a time.* After you have marked off the activities you don't enjoy and underlined the ones you care about most, look carefully

through the rest of the list. Circle at least three other activities you might be willing to sacrifice to gain family time at home. Then pick at least one (preferably more!) and mark it off your list right now. (If you have a Palm Pilot, take out that little thingamajig and start deleting.) Try to free up at least one afternoon or evening a week.

6. *Follow through with your cuts.* While you have your calendar out, be sure to schedule a time as soon as possible—within the week, at most—to make the phone calls and write the letters that remove you from obligations. This may be the hardest step of all—because people are bound to argue with you, and it might take a month or two to back out of certain involvements. Throughout this process, keep repeating to yourself *"Pick the best, say no to the rest."*

7. *Actually rehearse your no's.* If you are one of those people who really have trouble saying no, write out a list of gracious refusals and practice saying them in front of the mirror. Repeat over and over again, "Thanks for asking, but right now I need that time for my family." The more you say them, the more easily those words will come when you need them.

8. *Protect the time you've saved.* If you're like me, though, it's not enough to just cut items out of your family's schedule. If you leave places in your calendar blank, they are sure to fill up again quickly. To guard against that, it's not a bad idea to actually mark off blocks of time as "family time" or "down time" or "off limits" and refuse to schedule anything during those periods.

9. *Start a family tradition during the times you've roped off.* Some families choose a night of the week as "family night," when they play games and just hang out. Some

families enjoy Saturday mornings together. Others may rope off time before or after dinner—I've even heard of a family that enjoys "Happy Hour" (with snacks and drinks but no alcohol) in the late afternoons.

10. *Don't postpone joy!* In your quest to be a family that does less and sees one another more, don't overlook or postpone joyful living in the process. Rescheduling your schedule is probably going to take some time. In the meantime, make it a point to enjoy the times you do have with one another.

Strategy #12:
Adjust Your Attitude

I once heard speaker and author Donna Otto liken mothers to thermostats. She emphasized that our goal as mothers should be to "set the tone, the temperature" of our families rather than simply being thermometers that register the inevitable rise and fall of a family's attitudinal mercury. I liked that illustration. Instead of waiting for our children to change their attitudes—a loooong wait indeed!—let's work on adjusting our own and discover the pleasant effects of a loving, "not too cold and not too hot," but *just right*, atmosphere.

For me, the place to start when it comes to attitude is *contentment*. That means being satisfied with the things I have, the relationships in my life, and the reality of my life. The opposite of contentment, discontent, can rear its ugly head in many forms. Whenever I struggle with anger, resentment, envy, disappointment, or depression, I've had to ask myself, "Is the underlying reason for this feeling actually a lack of contentment?"

When I met my husband Rick, for instance, I was drawn to his quiet and easygoing sense of being. Okay, I was actually drawn to the 501 Levis he was wearing at the time, but the quiet presence came to my notice immediately afterward! I liked the fact that Rick thought through his responses before speaking. I liked the fact that Rick wanted to be with me pretty much all the time. I liked the fact that Rick was slim, dark, and handsome.

Then we got married. Around year seven I discovered I was far from content with either my marriage or Rick. It annoyed me that Rick thought through his responses before speaking. It annoyed me that Rick wanted to hang out at home with me and just me. It annoyed me that I had gained 30 pounds and he was still slim, dark, and handsome!

Probably every married woman has times when she's just not satisfied with her spouse. "If only he could dance," we gripe to ourselves. "If only he would stay home more." "If only he could get a better-paying job." "If only he would help me out more around the house." Some of our complaints are legitimate. Some aren't. But the reality under most of our "if onlys" is usually our own attitude of discontent—which eventually emerges in anger, resentment, comparison, and depression.

What about contentment with your children? Do you harbor resentment against them as you compare them to other children who are smarter, easier to handle, or more outgoing? Do you find yourself thinking: *If he could only be more coordinated. If she could only be prettier. If he could only stop wiggling so much. If only she weren't so shy.*

If, if, if, if—and the heart of the matter is that we are comparing our children to others or to some ideal and are discontent with the way they are. Mothers raising a child with special needs—be they physical, emotional, or mental—may find it especially difficult to say, "I am satisfied with my child just the way he or she is."

Almost all of us, regardless of our circumstances, struggle with discontent at one time or another. Divorced mothers may find themselves grumbling in the midst of custody procedures and stepparent realities. Single mothers may have difficulty accepting their singleness or their financial circumstances. Women who go to work may envy those who work at home—and vice versa.

Discontentment is actually a matter of attitude, not of circumstances. It really is possible to be a happy person in a shack or a muttering malcontent in a mansion. Being content is really a matter of accepting God's gift of who we are, where we are *right now*—without comparisons or "if onlys."

Do you remember the story in chapter 4 about my visit to the house of my new acquaintance, Stacey—how I was so overcome by jealousy at her beautiful house and by shame over my shabby one that I couldn't even relate to her? What shocked me the most about that entire situation was the ugly truth about my own covetous and envious nature. Coveting said, "I want what you have." Envy said, "I'm mad that I don't have what you have and I wish you didn't, either." And my own discontentment, the mother of those other two ugly attitudes, said, "If only my life were different…I could be happy."

Yuck! What a horrible way to feel! I begged God that day to teach me contentment. And though I'm still not immune to the "if onlys," I'm learning to adjust my attitude in the direction of contentment. Here are some ideas that have helped me:

Real Mom Points to Practice

1. *Remind yourself that God is the giver of all things—and He put you where you are for a purpose.* That means that your circumstances—your husband (or lack of one), your children, your job, your house—are all part of His plan for making you the person He wants you to be.

2. *Get a little perspective.* Our pastor once asked us to name aloud whom we considered "the rich." Most of us named Bill Gates and Ted Turner. The pastor went on to tell us that if we lived in a house with indoor plumbing, owned one vehicle, and had a television set, we were among the top 15 percent of the world in

wealth. If we lived in a home with central air condi-
tioning, owned two cars and two or more televisions,
we were in the top 5 percent. The point is, if we want
to discover true contentment, we might need to look
outside of our middle-class world.

3. *Volunteer to help someone less fortunate than you.* Serve
   soup at a homeless shelter, visit people in a nursing
   home, deliver Meals on Wheels, swing a hammer at a
   Habitat for Humanity house. If possible, involve your
   children with serving. You'll be surprised how helping
   others opens your eyes and changes your attitude.

4. *Practice giving thanks.* This is a good thing to do with
   your children. At least once a day, look around you and
   name at least five things in your life that you are thankful for. Some days you might need to be creative—
   "I'm thankful that the washing machine hasn't broken
   down in the last 24 hours." But there's nothing like an
   attitude of gratitude to help you feel more content.

5. *Ask yourself whether some of your discontent might have a
   purpose.* Feelings of restlessness or dissatisfaction
   could be a sign that you need to make some changes
   in your life. I don't mean leaving your husband or
   children—though the idea may be tempting!

   Maybe it is time to change your routine. Go to the
   early service at church instead of the late one. Pull out
   your cookbooks and make something new for dinner.
   Sit down at the piano and pull out the music you
   haven't touched in a year and a half. Instead of
   whining "if only"...try something new!

Strategy #13:
Find a Godly Role Model

When I was a young girl, I used to attend the Church of God, Holiness in Moberly, Missouri, with my beloved grandparents. I can close my eyes and instantly find myself sitting four pews from the front row, organ side. My grandparents, Cecil and Bonnie Patrick, loved to watch Nola Johnson work the keyboard and make that plain, simple organ sing like a baby grand at a Jerry Lee Lewis concert.

Sitting near us would be Brother and Sister Pugh—the pastor and his wife. Sister Pugh styled her hair in the same "sister" fashion as the other older female members of our denomination. I call it the Tower of Babel look—high and unto heaven! For those of you who never attended a Holiness meeting during the early 1970s, the unspoken motto was: "The higher the hair, the closer to heaven." Sister Pugh was knocking at the front gates. Most Sundays I would try to puzzle out which bobby pin, if removed, would bring the entire bun tumbling down like the walls of Jericho.

I never did see a skirt line that exposed a knee in that church, nor did any women represent Mary Kay products. I suppose some would say they were "good" Christians because of their modesty and "churchy" style. But did their hair or clothing make them godly? No. What set these women and my grandmother apart was their manner of showing the love of Christ to their families and to those around them.

As a five-year-old I used to sit with Grandma in a red Falcon station wagon on steaming July afternoons. We would sit and wait as an older woman named Jewel purchased her groceries at the local store, and then we would drive her to various places so she could pay monthly bills. Grandma also cared lovingly for countless foster kids and once drove an old, flop-eared German shepherd to a vet in tears, fearing a less-than-optimistic prognosis.

Throughout the years she did many good deeds. Even more important, she allowed the tenderness and the compassion of her Savior Jesus Christ to permeate her daily life. It is from her that I learned most of my lessons in what it means to be a godly woman—from her teaching, but most of all from her example. It was my grandma's heart that God had hold of, and until her last breath, on March 22, 1994, her life bore the eternal fingerprints of God. And my life, in turn, has her fingerprints all over it. I can't claim to be the world's best mother or the world's best Christian, but so much of what I've become is because of the influence of that godly woman, my first role model.

Throughout my life at different intervals God has demonstrated His love for me by providing a godly woman I could learn from. After moving to Bushnell, Illinois, I got to know Gayla English, and I was amazed at how she enjoyed, even *liked*, being together with her (then) three daughters. They were inseparable.

I, on the other hand, had to learn to love being a family. Rick and I had only ten months together as a married couple when Kristen came along. A year later, I found myself expecting Ricky Neal. Oh, I loved my children and I enjoyed being a mother but…I still saw my life as "we" versus "me"—and I wanted to be "me" a lot more than a "we."

Now, I'm never going to be just like Gayla. My temperament is quite different, and God has different plans for each of our families. Thanks to her influence, however, I have become more of a "love me, love my family" mother. My heart doesn't desire to be so independent as it did eight years ago. When I leave for an overnight or weekend engagement, I find myself getting homesick a lot sooner.

That, my friend, is a miraculous change of heart for this "lead, follow, or get out of my way" woman!

I have learned that loving my children is a choice. Godly friends like Debbie Schade and Tina Mueller have encouraged me to *choose* to love and to *choose* to be kind and sensitive toward my children. Often I would have preferred to respond differently, but their examples and teachings impacted my thinking. I shudder to think of the mother I might have been without them.

Initiate a Relationship

Four years ago I was struggling with some completely new issues. While anger was not so much a problem with my children anymore, I had begun to resent my inability to pursue public speaking full-time. Ever since high school I had known I needed to be a speaker, and now, quite frankly, I was beginning to tire of waiting. I had worked through past anger issues. I had come to enjoy my children, and I reveled in parenting our third child, Patrick Michael. Yet, I could sense the warning signs, and I knew I had to deal with my edginess and impatience quickly…or find myself back to square one.

This time I approached Gwen, an older woman in my church who had daughters my age. I had watched her at church camp the year before as she worked as senior counselor with the nine- and ten-year-old girls. What a beautiful example I saw in Gwen! The tender manner in which she handled a homesick child and her honest confession of being hot and uncomfortable had won me over completely by day four.

On a Wednesday evening after Bible study I asked Gwen if she would consider being my mentor. I explained I needed someone with "been there" experience to talk to about these new emotions of discontent and frustration. We began meeting just a few days later. I don't recall either of us saying anything extremely profound. It wasn't a matter of her quoting just the right Scriptures or telling me what I should do. I didn't magically stop struggling with the when, where, and what of a speaking career. However, I did find a safe place to pour out my frustrations over juggling a passionate God-given vision for public speaking and the God-given responsibilities to my husband and children.

We met for a rather short time, yet I believe with all my heart that this book and all the details that have fallen into place over the past five years are a direct result of listening to Gwen's sage and godly advice. Because of her counsel, I did not let go of the eternal (my family) for the temporal (a few extra years of speaking).

I want to encourage you to actively pursue a relationship such as this. Mothers thrive in the nurturing environment of mentoring relationships with godly, experienced mothers. Perhaps you are a bit like me and find it difficult to admit you need a little "leadership" in this area of your life. After all, aren't we supposed to just know how to be a "good" mother? Don't allow pride or insecurity to keep you from seeking out a relationship with someone who can be strong in your area of weakness and shine some "been there" experience on the issues you face with your children. Behind every great mother there is a prayer warrior and a friend.

It's not always necessary to initiate a formal relationship. Often you can learn by just being around and observing mothers you admire. But actually asking an experienced, godly mother to act as your mentor for a period of time can be immensely rewarding.

If the idea of initiating this kind of contact makes you a bit jittery, consider asking a close friend or women's leader within your church to approach the mother you have in mind with the idea. After picking herself up off the floor (remember, we all tend to remember our failures, not our successes), she may want more details. How much time do you want to spend together? What type of issues are you dealing with? Be ready to express your needs clearly and don't forget to *pray*. God will put you together with just the right mother and personality.

Real Mom Points to Practice

1. *Think back through your early life.* Can you think of some godly women you have known whose example you could follow today? What qualities did they show that you would like in your own life? Write these down on a sheet of paper and make them a subject for prayer.

2. *List the needs or struggles that you have as a mother.* Pray specifically that God would send you a friend or mentor who understands those needs and can help you grow.

3. *Write down the names of three older women you know who seem to have done a pretty decent job of raising their families.* Choose women who are several years older than you. When working with a mentor, you need the perspective that only time and experience can give. Begin praying, and ask God if one of these women might be a good choice to serve as your mentor. In the meantime, watch these women in action and observe what they do.

4. *Break out of your age comfort zones.* Involve yourself in organizations, ministries, and friendships in which you can have contact with women both older and younger than yourself. The Sunday school class I'm now teaching has women from age 19 to age 81. It's

been a wonderful source of learning, encouragement, and flat-out fun to listen to such a varied and broad base of experience.

5. *As you grow in your mothering skills, consider being a mentor or friend to a younger mother.* You don't have to be perfect in order to help someone else. And you may find that the act of mentoring a younger woman helps you grow in godliness yourself.

6. *Turn to the Bible for other examples of godly women.* Why not get together with your friends and do a study of Proverbs 31 or of mothers in the Bible?

Strategy #14:
Start a Support Group

We all need a safety valve, especially during those scary times when anger seems to blind us to anything sensible. So here's a simple, practical strategy that can help make a difference in your life and the lives of other mothers around you. Help form a "Code: I'm Gonna Blow" support group with three or four other mothers who could also benefit from accountability and practical assistance concerning anger and children.

This doesn't have to be an arduous task. It can be as simple as calling three friends or posting a note on a church or YMCA bulletin board. You might write a message similar to this; "Do you tend to 'blow it' in anger with your kids? If you'd like to be a part of a small support group of moms who encourage one another and are willing to be there for each other when times are tough, then call me at _____."

This isn't just a discussion group—it's a lifesaving group. "Code: I'm Gonna Blow" is your key phrase to signal one another that you need help...now! Members should agree to do what is necessary to help the "blow-er" calm down. Perhaps one mom will watch another's child while the first mom drives around or walks around the block six or seven *hundred* times! One mom might "talk down" another mom over the phone. All group members should be ready to remind each other that their children are blessings, not burdens.

Make your battle cry short and sweet. "I'm gonna blow!" should say it all! The caller can make her immediate needs known, whether she might need a calming phone conversation or a place to leave the kids for awhile. She should call when the intensity of anger and rage first begins to build.

"Code: I'm Gonna Blow!" can also provide a confidential avenue to discuss trigger points and "underground" issues within your lives as moms. Without question, the women involved must honor one another with absolute confidentiality and lovingly hold one another accountable for changes in their behavior. It's so much easier to work with someone than to work alone.

Real Mom Points to Practice

1. *Limit the "Code" group's size to three or four and agree to meet once or twice a month.* If you all chip in, you should be able to afford a babysitter to watch the kids—or park them all at a well-run Mother's Day Out.

2. *Maintain absolute confidentiality with one another.* Letting other moms see you at what you think is your worst is difficult and requires trust on the part of those participating. It's vital that each group member honor the trust the others have put in her.

3. *Read about moms just like you at <parentsplace.com>.* Go to "Boards" and click on "Anger Management." The mothers at this message board are real and understand anger towards children. Nothing replaces human contact, but if you're in a pinch or find yourself climbing the walls at 2:45 A.M. with a colicky baby, this can be quite encouraging.

The Way We Are

Quite honestly, I'm amazed at the job I've done as a mom.

In light of the fact that I once sat Kristen—in her punkin' seat—on the roof of a Mazda Spyder and nearly *(nearly!)* drove off before remembering her, I think it's quite extraordinary that all my children are not only alive but toilet-trained, up-to-date on their vaccines, adequately clothed, and able to tie their own shoes. Since that amazing day that Kristen arrived, I've messed up, goofed up, and flat-out done things wrong, but boy, have I done some things right. Like holding my babies when most everyone said, "Let them cry themselves to sleep." Or like playing big-band swing music *way* too loud, *far* too late in the evening, and dancing with my nine-year-old son while his four-year-old brother fell over laughing.

These memories are too sacred to be shared with just anyone…but you, my dear reader, are not just anyone. You are a mother just like me. You have experienced the thrill and agony of breathing and pushing in a hospital delivery room, or anxiously pacing at the end of an airport terminal, or standing by a quiet telephone, waiting to receive word or confirmation of *your* baby's delivery into your waiting arms and heart.

You aren't just anyone. You are a mother just like me.

You had high ideals. You knew what you would *never* do, no matter what; and you have watched many of those ideals come crashing down and pile up in a heap of reality around your Cheerio-encrusted toes!

But take heart, dear friend. There is light at the end of the tunnel...and this time it's not an annoying blue engine named Thomas! No, this light of hope is the loving and satisfying relationship that you and your child will experience as a result of your acknowledging Mount Momma and dealing with your anger.

This summer, while watching Ricky Neal play Little League baseball, I suddenly found myself crying. I realized that I no longer mulled over the dark truths of my early parenting years. I no longer went to bed regretting my children's existence—and mine. I no longer was eaten up with guilt...such awful guilt. I loved all three of my children, and I enjoyed being a mother to them.

Kristen is now twelve, Ricky Neal is ten, and Patrick is five, and we have experienced joy and laughter in our home for many years now. In fact, after I read this manuscript aloud to the kids, Patrick asked me, "Where're all my stories, Mom?"

"Well, Patrick," I explained, "by the time you came along, Mom knew what she was doing a little bit better."

He pouted a few moments and then hugged me and said, "Mom, I love you more than pigs and ice cream!" and ran off to do what little boys do.

Well, I must have done something right, don't you think?

Hearts Entrusted

These tiny hearts to me entrusted,
Soft and tender,
Pockets of soil moist with innocence,
Laden with surprises,
Giggles,
Questions,
Love.
With one blast of anger,
One word unkindly spoken,
One glare of intolerance,
I can cause these tiny hearts to…
Fear,
Cower,
Or—God forbid—
Hate.
I want to plant within their souls seeds of…
Joy,
Contentment,

Love
heaping
upon
love.
Yet, thorny briers of...
Harshness,
Impatience,
Bitterness,
I have heedlessly allowed to grow.
Remorseful?
Yes.
Able to call back?
Never.
Forgiven?
Oh yes, more than I deserve.
Lord, I don't want to fail again.
May I be found faithful to these created by You.
Praise for A-B-Cs perfected,
"Thank you," for windows cleansed with Pledge.
There are no second chances.
I cannot undo the past.
Jesus,
Sear my heart with love and devotion.
May I be a sower of seeds,
A shelter amidst the storm.
May I hear,
"Well done, good and faithful mother."
May I be found true.

Acknowledgments

My husband—Rick: For always believing this book would be, and patiently listening as I read each page aloud—again and again and again.

My children—Kristen, Ricky Neal, and Patrick: Nothing I hear compares to hearing you say "love you, Mom" as you breeze through the house. Nothing I do will ever be as momentous as the final push that brought each of you into the welcoming arms of your daddy and me. Nothing I write will mean as much as the scribbled notes and stick-figure drawings that hang along our stairwell wall. I love you forever; I'll like you for always—I'm so glad I'm your mom.

My parents—Norman and Jean Patrick: For the priceless gift of growing up treasured, loved, and wanted. Surely my love for books comes from the many hours of being read to as a child and the thrill of opening a brown package labeled "Weekly Reader Book Club." Making you laugh—and making you proud in the process—has been my ambition since age three!

My extended family—Ronald, Jeannie, and Tammie Barnhill; Rod and Dona Barnhill; and Mark and Trisha Lowman: You have made this so much easier by entertaining the kids when they were sick of seeing their mom in front of a keyboard. I'm so glad the kids have grandparents and uncles and aunts that enjoy them and take them camping and trout fishing during deadline time. The kids and Rick and I love you very much—with or without the campers!

Junior and Cynthia Holtmeyer and Barbara Barry: Junior and Cynthia—coffee table books, chip-n-dip, story hour, Easter eggs, Chocolate Soldier pop, and piggyback rides on Junior's strong back. B.B.—a box of hidden treasures at your old apartment, grown-up conversations at age six, and all those wonderful knick-knacks you let me touch! You have loved me as your own and regarded my children in the same way. I love you all dearly!

Mrs. Dorothy Glenn: My favorite teacher (Brunswick Elementary, grade two) *of all time* who instilled within me a love for reading and a passion for writing—but not phonics! I never would have graduated from the "bluebird" reading group without you!

Bill and Jo Greene: As a seven-year-old child I watched you as a married couple and determined to marry only a man whose face lit up when I entered a room and who laughed at my jokes. I did. Thank you for the marvelous example!

Audrey Denney-Reischauer: You are the Ethel to my Lucy! You *get* my warped perspective on life and, what's scarier… you often agree. Staying up until four in the morning reading the Word of God—who else but you could read the book of Leviticus and find humor in leprosy? Ranting and raving about injustice, evil, and stale Oreos. Listening without judgment as I unloaded maternal sorrows and regret. Every woman needs a girlfriend like you! Now get that conference lined up in Florida so I can come down and see you!

Charlene Ann Baumbich: While laughing my head off listening to you at a Hearts at Home conference, I knew I had to get to know you. Here at last was a speaker I could relate to, someone who revealed her frailties and public missteps with authenticity and a potent dose of humor—lots of humor! For the past few years, you have been the "kick in the pants" that this clueless novice so desperately needed. I would not be writing this or any other book without your support and recommendation three years ago to Hearts at Home. It is a privilege to call you both friend and colleague.

Jill Savage and the dedicated women of Hearts at Home: Your commitment to moms is incredible! Thank you for allowing me an opportunity to share my vision with the spring conference attendees in 1998. I never imagined the great things that would come as a result...keep on doing what you are doing for the glory of God.

Margie Thompson: You listened to me go on and on about my passion to speak and write and then sat stunned weeks later as I told you, "I'm going to apply for a full-time pharmaceutical sales position." What?! Immediately you e-mailed me and urged, "Mail that book proposal and just see what happens!" I did and look what happened! Your commitment to excellence in all things inspires me to think harder, work longer, and keep going for my dream.

Lisa Schafer: You found my lost manuscript floating somewhere between "My Documents" and "Explorer." I thank God for analytical and computer-competent friends like you!

The Harvest House publishing team: Carolyn McCready and LaRae Weikert, who made me feel like a welcomed friend over a four-hour lunch in March of last year—with simple and transparent conversations about ourselves and our passion to serve Christ—all the start of a wonderful working relationship. Barb Sherrill, who read my very rough draft and proposal and ran with it. How many authors in Illinois have the pleasure of serving Sunday lunch to one of their editors from Oregon? God works in the most exquisite and marvelous ways! Betty Fletcher, who assured me, "You will write a fabulous book!"

Anne Christian Buchanan, who understands the Anne Lamott theory of first drafts and led me skillfully and gently—we first-time authors are a sensitive lot—through my first-time experience with editing. I could not have done this without you. I can't wait to do it all again!

Most of all, *the mothers who have shared with me their fears and struggles:* You will remain firmly in my heart and prayers long after this book has seen its day. Your names have been changed and some minor details have been left out, but your stories of anger and sorrow are engraved on every page. You were the crucial ingredient in my completing something that rings true. For those I have wept with or listened to over the phone, thank you for trusting me with your hearts. This book is *our* testimony…we are not alone!

Appendixes

Help, Resources, and Information

Could You Be Depressed?

Symptoms and Resources

If you are really struggling with an ongoing problem of anger toward your children, you might be suffering from depression or some other form of mental or emotional disorder. This doesn't mean you're "crazy." It certainly doesn't mean that you have failed as a mother or a Christian. It could, however, make it harder for you to handle your anger toward your children. And it might well require some kind of professional help if you're going to get better.

The subject of depression—and the fact that it afflicts many of God's people—is largely ignored within the Christian culture. In church prayer meetings we are quick to request a prayer for physical healing but seldom, if ever, does anyone request a prayer for mental healing or even share his or her struggles in this area. This is understandable, because many Christians still attach a stigma to the problem of mental illness. Fellow believers may imply that if a person were "stronger in character," or if he or she "had enough faith," the mental illness would just go away. Sincere—yet sincerely wrong—believers have even suggested that mental illness is *simply* a result of unconfessed sin or the work of demonic forces.

Both of these ideas are dangerous. Depression, anxiety, dysthymia (long-term chronic symptoms that do not disable you, but keep you from feeling "good"), manic-depressive illness (also known as bipolar disorder), and schizophrenia are all very real disorders, often with a physical cause, and the consequences of ignoring them or brushing them aside with a trite Christian phrase can be traumatic indeed. And seeking help from a medical doctor, a mental health facility, a Christian counselor, or all of them can be an important step toward healing.

If you have suffered or are suffering from any of the following symptoms for more than two weeks at a time, please consider seeking professional counsel. (This is *not* an all-inclusive list!) If you have any questions or concerns, consult with your physician.

- persistent sad, anxious, or "empty" mood
- feelings of hopelessness or pessimism
- feelings of guilt, worthlessness, or helplessness
- loss of interest or pleasure in hobbies and activities that were once enjoyed, including sex
- insomnia, early-morning awakening, or oversleeping
- loss of appetite or weight loss or both—or overeating and weight gain
- decreased energy, fatigue, a feeling of being "slowed down"
- thoughts of death or suicide; suicide attempts
- restlessness or irritability
- difficulty concentrating, remembering things, or making decisions

- persistent physical symptoms that do not respond to treatment—such as headaches, digestive disorders, and chronic pain

Where Can You Find Help?

Listed below are the types of people and places that will give you a referral to diagnostic and treatment services or provide them for you.

- family doctors
- mental health specialists, such as psychiatrists, psychologists, social workers, or mental health counselors
- health maintenance organizations
- community mental health centers
- hospital psychiatry departments and outpatient clinics
- programs affiliated with universities or medical schools
- state hospital outpatient clinics
- family service/social agencies
- private clinics and facilities
- employee assistance programs
- local medical or psychiatric societies

Check the Yellow Pages under mental health, health, social services, suicide prevention, hospitals, or physicians for phone numbers and addresses in your local area.

Note: If you just can't summon the energy to check out these resources, that *in itself* might be a sign that you are depressed. Ask a friend or your spouse to help you. It's important!

Resources and Recommended Reading

Here are my recommendations of resources and reading material on a wide variety of topics. I think you'll enjoy researching and discovering the vast array of material that is available to us mothers. I pray that these sources will help you in your taming of Mount Momma. Just don't blow your top when the children ask you to put down that book or get off the computer for awhile!

General Parenting Resources

Arrington, Lael. *Worldproofing Your Kids: Helping Moms Prepare Their Kids to Navigate Today's Turbulent Times.* Wheaton, IL: Crossway Books, 1997. Lael is an incredible thinker and is able to put those "big" thoughts into a very readable and useful resource for mothers. This is a must-have book!

Focus on the Family. Website at <www.fotf.org>. Can also be reached at 8605 Explorer Dr., Colorado Springs, CO 80920; Voice: 719-531-3400 or Fax: 719-531-3341. Founded by Dr. James Dobson. A wonderful resource on marriage, parenting, and all subjects relating to family life.

Gaither, Gloria, ed. *What My Parents Did Right*. Nashville: Star Song Publishing, 1991. Encouragement and food for thought as you read what famous people say about the "right" things their parents did that shaped their lives.

Leach, Penelope. *Your Baby and Child: From Birth to Age Five*. New York: Alfred A. Knopf, 1987.

Miller, Kathy Collard, and Darcy Miller. *Staying Friends with Your Kids*. Wheaton, IL: Harold Shaw, 1997.

Mulder, Robyn. *The Robyn's Nest*. URL=<http://members.truepath.com/TheNest/TheNest.html>. A friendly and *real* site written for mothers by a mother.

Parents Place. A general parenting website at <www.parentsplace.com>. There is something of interest for everyone at this place—and too many message boards to even count!

Rosemond, John. *A Family of Value*. Kansas City, MO: Andrews McMeel Publishing, 1995. This book was out of stock the last time I checked at Amazon.com but can be found in public libraries. I love the "common sense" approach toward parenting and children that Mr. Rosemond emphasizes.

Simon, Mary Manz. *How to Parent Your "Tweenager"— Understanding the In-Between Years of Your 8–12 Year Old*. Nashville: Thomas Nelson, 1995. This title was also out of stock at Amazon.com, but it's an excellent resource; I encourage you to find it wherever you can!

Parenting Spirited/High-Need Children

Gallagher, Teresa. *Born to Explore! The Other Side of ADD*. Website at <borntoexplore.org/index.html>. An excellent site!

Gibson, Elaine. *The Challenge of Difficult Children: Elaine M. Gibson's Insights on Parenting.* Accessed at <www.smu.edu/~egibson>. An excellent resource for understanding "difficult" children. Be sure to click on "About the Author" and read her "been there, still there" story.

Kurcinka, Mary Sheedy. *Raising Your Spirited Child: A Guide for Parents Whose Child Is More Intense, Sensitive, Perceptive, Persistent, and Energetic.* New York: Harper Perennial, 1991, 1998. A must-have—also available as a workbook and book on tape.

Nurturing Our Spirited Children: The Online Resource for Parenting Spirited, High Need, or Difficult Children. Accessed at <www.nurturingourfamilies.com/spirited/index.html>. Click on "Online Resources—Information and Support" for listings of invaluable interactive support forums for parents of "high-spirited/high-need" children. Includes various moderated and unmoderated message boards, chat rooms, e-mail list, and so on.

Palladino, Lucy Jo. *The Edison Trait: Saving the Spirit of Your Nonconforming Child.* New York: Times Books, 1997.

Sensory Comfort: Making Life More Comfortable for Children and Adults with Sensory Processing Differences. Website accessed at <www.sensorycomfort.com>. This website is a great source of information about kids who react differently to sensory stimulation. It also sells a variety of helpful products for high-sensitivity kids, including seamless socks.

Solutions for Sensitive Feet. Website at <www.sensitivefeet.com/sensitivefeet/cricseamsocf.html>. An online source for Cricket Seamless Socks for kids. These great socks are wonderful for high-sensitivity kids. The socks

can also be ordered via mail, voice, or fax from Healthy
Legs and Feet Too!, 6333 SW Macadam Ave., Suite 102,
Portland, OR 97201; Voice: 888-495-0105 (available
M–F, 9 A.M.–6 P.M., and Saturdays 10 A.M.–4 P.M. PST);
Fax: 503-245-2441 (available 24 hours a day).

Stacinator. Website at: <www.stacinator.com/order.html>.
A source of hand-sewn fleece diaper covers for your
high-sensitivity little ones.

Turecki, Stanley, with Leslie Tonner. *The Difficult Child*, 2nd
rev. ed. New York: Bantam Doubleday Dell, 2000.
Another must-have for moms hoping to understand
their "difficult" children. Encouraging and enlightening!

Humor

Baumbich, Charlene Ann. *Mama Said There'd Be Days Like
This: But She Never Said Just How Many*. Ann Arbor, MI:
Vine Books, 1995.

Baumbich, Charlene Ann. *The Book of Duh*. Wheaton, IL:
Harold Shaw, 1997.

Higgs, Liz Curtis. *Mirror, Mirror on the Wall, Have I Got
News for You!: An A to Z Faith Lift for Your Sagging Self-
Esteem*. Nashville: Thomas Nelson, 1997.

Freeman, Becky. *The Best of Becky Freeman*. New York:
Inspirational Press, 1998.

Positive and Effective Discipline

Leman, Kevin. *Making Children Mind Without Losing Yours*.
Old Tappan, NJ: Fleming H. Revell, 1984.

Leman, Kevin. *Bringing Up Kids Without Tearing Them
Down: How to Raise Confident, Successful Children*.
Nashville: Thomas Nelson, 1995.

Positive Discipline, Inc. Accessed at
    <www.positivediscipline.com>. Offers workshops,
    classes, and advice for parents and teachers nation-
    wide.

Children and Anger

Eastman, Meg, and Sydney Craft Rozen. *Taming the
    Dragon in Your Child: Solutions for Breaking the Cycle of
    Family Anger.* New York: John Wiley & Sons, 1994.

Children and Stress

Elkind, David. *The Hurried Child: Growing Up Too Fast, Too
    Soon.* Cambridge, MA: Perseus Press, 1989. A revised
    edition of this book became available February 2001.

Hart, Archibald. *Stress and Your Child.* Dallas, TX: Word,
    1994. Good help from a Christian psychologist.

Temperaments

Keirsey Temperament and Character Web Site. Accessed at
    <www.keirsey.com>. A different approach to
    temperament, similar to (but not the same as) the
    widely used Myers-Briggs Type Indicator. At this
    website you can use an online "personality sorter"
    and read helpful information on how temperaments
    relate to parenting.

Littauer, Florence. *Personality Plus: How to Understand
    Others by Understanding Yourself,* revised ed. Old
    Tappan, NJ: Fleming H. Revell, 1992. This is Florence
    Littauer's original bestseller about temperaments.

Littauer, Florence. *Personality Plus for Parents: Under-
    standing What Makes Your Child Tick.* Grand Rapids, MI:
    Fleming H. Revell, 2000.

Littauer, Florence. *Your Personality Tree.* Dallas, TX: Word, 1989. Delves deeper into the temperaments and why we sometimes mask our true temperament.

Miller, Donna J., and Linda Holland. *Growing Little Women: Capturing Teachable Moments with Your Daughter.* Chicago: Moody Press, 1997. This is an excellent resource to help moms mentor their daughters. I've learned many things about my own daughter as we've worked through the book.

Trent, John T. *The Treasure Tree.* Dallas, TX: Word, 1994. An adorable book for kids (and adults) about how people of different temperaments can learn to understand themselves and each other and work together.

Women and Anger

Miller, Kathy Collard. "I Abused My Child: One Mother's Story," *Christian Parenting*, January/February 2000, pp. 26-30. This is the lone article I found in which a Christian mother admitted to uncontrolled anger and abuse.

Oliver, Gary J., and H. Norman Wright. *Pressure Points: Women Speak Out About Their Anger at Life's Demands.* Chicago: Moody Press, 1993.

Oliver, Gary J., and H. Norman Wright. *Good Women Get Angry: A Woman's Guide to Handling Her Anger, Depression, Anxiety, and Stress.* Ann Arbor, MI: Vine Books, 1995.

Samalin, Nancy, and Catherine Whitney. *Love and Anger: The Parental Dilemma.* New York: Penguin, 1995.

Emotional/Mental Health Issues for Women

Lush, Jean, Julia Lush, and Patricia H. Rushford. *Emotional Phases of a Woman's Life.* Old Tappan, NJ: Fleming H. Revell, 1990.

Mintle, Linda. *Getting Unstuck*. Orlando, FL: Creation House, 1999.

Poinsett, Brenda. *Why Do I Feel This Way?: What Every Women Needs to Know about Depression*. Colorado Springs, CO: NavPress, 1996.

National Foundation for Depressive Illness. PO Box 2257, New York, NY 10116, 1-800-239-1265. Website at <www.depression.org/index.html>.

National Depressive and Manic Depressive Association. 730 N. Franklin St., Suite 501, Chicago, IL 60610-3526; Voice: 1-800-826-3632 or 1-312-642-0049; Fax: 1-312-642-7243. Website at: <www.ndmda.org>.

National Mental Health Association. 1021 Prince St., Alexandria, VA 22314-2971. Call the Mental Health Information Center at 1-800-969-6642 (TTY Line: 1-800-433-5959) or access at <www.nmha.org>.

Resnick, Susan Kushner. *Sleepless Days: One Woman's Journey Through Postpartum Depression*. New York: St. Martin's Press, 1999.

Sichel, Deborah, and Jeanne Watson Driscoll. *Women's Moods: What Every Woman Must Know About Hormones, the Brain, and Emotional Health*. New York: William Morrow, 1999.

Waggoner, Brenda, and Becky Freeman. *The Velveteen Woman: Becoming Real Through God's Transforming Love*. Colorado Springs, CO: Chariot Victor, 1999.

Dealing with Your Past

Eldridge, Sherrie. *Twenty Things Adopted Kids Wish Their Adoptive Parents Knew*. New York: Dell Books, 1999.

Farmer, Steven. *Adult Children of Abusive Parents: A Healing Program for Those Who Have Been Abused*

Physically, Sexually, or Emotionally. New York: Ballantine Books, 1990.

Heitritter, Lynn, and Jeanette Vought. *Helping Victims of Sexual Abuse: A Sensitive, Biblical Guide for Counselors, Victims, and Families.* Minneapolis: Bethany House, 1989.

Jewel Among Jewels Adoption Network. Accessed at <www.adoptionjewels.org>; E-mail: <mail@adoptionjewels.org>; Voice: 317-849-5651; Fax: 317-915-8636. This network seeks to celebrate the sovereignty of God in the act of adoption, educate people about the possible repercussions of relinquishment, and encourage each person touched by adoption to embrace as well as enjoy God's opinion of him or her—a jewel among jewels.

Pelzer, David J. *A Child Called "It": An Abused Child's Journey from Victim to Victor.* Deerfield Beach, FL: Health Communications, 1995.

Pelzer, David J. *A Man Named Dave: A Story of Triumph and Forgiveness.* New York: E.P. Dutton, 1999.

Wright, H. Norman. *Making Peace with Your Past.* Grand Rapids, MI: Baker Book House, 1997.

Single Mothers

Jakes, T. D. *Help! I'm Raising My Children Alone: A Guide for Single Parents and Those Who Sometimes Feel They Are.* Orlando, FL: Creation House, 1996.

McCoy, Jonni. "Miserly Moms Resources for Single Moms." Accessed at <www.miserlymoms.com/MOMsmoms.htm>. This page on the Miserly Moms website will link you with articles and organizations that are of special interest to single moms.

Osborn, Susan Titus, Lucille Moses, and John T. Trent. *Rest Stops for Single Moms: Encouragement for the Journey.* Nashville: Broadman & Holman, 2000.

At-Home Mothers

Hearts at Home. 900 W. College Avenue, Normal, IL 61761; Voice: 309-888-6667; Fax: 309-888-4525; E-mail: <hearts@dave-world.net>. Accessed at <www.hearts-at-home.org>. This fabulous organization offers conferences throughout the United States where mothers can meet their favorite authors and speakers as they attend educational workshops that strengthen their hearts and homes. You won't want to miss a conference in your area!

Otto, Donna. *The Stay-at-Home Mom.* Eugene, OR: Harvest House, 1997.

Working Mothers

Welchel, Mary. "The Christian Working Woman." PO Box 1210, Wheaton, IL 60189; Voice: 630-462-0552; Fax: 630-462-1613. Accessed at <www.christianworkingwoman.org>. Mary Welchel is a radio host, author, and speaker who offers lots of useful information for the Christian working woman (including moms) of the new millennium.

Mentoring Resources

Cagle, Judy. "Renewal through Mentoring," *APEO Renewal Manual.* Laguna Hills, CA: Asia Pacific Education Office, 1998. Accessed at <www.apeo.org/general-renew/chap7.htm>. Unsure how to find a mentor? Feeling a little clueless as to what to expect from one and from yourself? This concise and thorough article will point you in the right direction.

Hunt, Susan. *Spiritual Mothering: The Titus 2 Model for Women Mentoring Women.* Wheaton, IL: Crossway Books, 1993.

Johnson, Erik. "How to Be an Effective Mentor," *Leadership Journal,* vol. 21. no. 2 (spring 2000), p. 36. Accessed at <www.christianitytoday.com/le/2000/002/5.36.html>. This article offers practical information for those who may not be sure what to expect in a mentoring relationship. Use it as a resource while developing your own expectations and questions for your future mentor—as well as a guide for being an effective mentor yourself.

Kent, Carol. *Becoming a Woman of Influence: Making a Lasting Impact on Others.* Colorado Springs, CO: NavPress, 1999.

Otto, Donna. *Between Women of God.* Eugene, OR: Harvest House Publishers, 1995.

Otto, Donna. *The Gentle Art of Mentoring.* Eugene, OR: Harvest House Publishers, 1997.

Finances

McCoy, Jonni. *Miserly Moms.* Elkton, MD: Holly Hall Publications, 1996. The Miserly Moms website at <www.miserlymoms.com> is full of great ideas for living frugally.

Hunt, Mary. *Mary Hunt's Debt-Proof Living.* Nashville: Broadman & Holman, 1999. You can visit Mary Hunt's website at <www.cheapsk8.com> for information about her radio program and newsletter as well as for helpful advice.

Frugal Gazette. Accessed at <www.frugalgazette.com>. This is another helpful "frugal" site that offers the opportunity to subscribe to a newsletter.

Bibles, Inspirational Books, and Devotionals for Moms and Children

Moms

God's Little Devotional Bible for Women. Tulsa, OK: Honor Books, 1998.

KJV Mother's Bible. Iowa Falls, IA: World Bible Publishers, 1996.

Lotz, Anne Graham. *Just Give Me Jesus*. Dallas: Word Books, 2000.

Miller, Kathy Collard. *God's Abundance for Women: Devotions for a More Meaningful Life*. Lancaster, PA: Starburst Publishers, 1999.

NIV Mom's Devotional Bible. Grand Rapids, MI: Zondervan Publishing House, 1997.

NIV Recovery Devotional Bible. Grand Rapids, MI: Zondervan Publishing House, 1993.

Schneiders, Kali. *Truffles from Heaven: Discovering the Sweet of God's Grace*. Colorado Springs, CO: Chariot Victor, 1999.

Wheeler, Joe L. *Heart to Heart: Stories for Moms*. Wheaton, IL: Tyndale House, 2000. A collection of stories about the many faces of mother love.

Babies and Toddlers

Baby's First Bible, King James Version. Nashville: Thomas Nelson, 1985.

The Beginner's Bible for Toddlers. Dallas, TX: Word Publishing, 1995.

Beers, V. Gilbert. *The Toddler's Bible*. Colorado Springs, CO: Chariot Victor, 1992.

Children 4–8

Hochstatter, Daniel J. (illustrator) and Daryl J. Lucas. *The Eager Reader Bible: Bible Stories to Grow On.* Wheaton, IL: Tyndale House, 1999.

Precious Moments Bible, Contemporary English Version. Nashville: NelsonWord Publishing Group, 1996.

Children 9–12

Adventure Bible, Revised, NIV. Grand Rapids, MI: Zondervan Publishing House, 2000.

Miralles, Joseph (illustrator), Stephen R. Covey, J. Grispino. *Golden Children's Bible: The Old and New Testaments.* Crawfordsville, IN: Golden Books Publishing, 1993.

The One Year Bible for Kids: Greatest Bible Passages Arranged in 365 Daily Readings, New Living Translation. Wheaton, IL: Tyndale House Publishing, 1997.

Teens and Young Adults

Thompson Student Bible, New International Version. Indianapolis, IN: Kirkbride, 1999.

Student's Life Application Bible, New Living Translation. Wheaton, IL: Tyndale House Publishing, 1997.

McDowell, Josh, ed., *The Rock: The Bible for Making Right Choices, New Living Translation.* Wheaton, IL: Tyndale House, 1998.

Online Resources for Bible Study and Strengthening Your Faith

Crosswalk.Com Bible Study Tools. Accessed at <www.bible.crosswalk.com>. Incredible access to commentaries, dictionaries, concordances, and other free tools. I use this site all the time!

Ravi Zacharias International Ministries. *Let My People Think* program archive. Accessed at <www.gospelcom.net/rzim/ra_program_archive.htm>. RealAudio Sure Stream access to the teachings of apologist Ravi Zacharias. His speaking will challenge you and help you become a discerning woman and mother.

Christianity Today Bible and Reference.Com. Accessed at <www.christianitytoday.com/bible/>. Another resource for online Bible study, in conjunction with *Christianity Today* magazine.

Gospel Communications Network Online Christian Resources. Accessed at <www.gospelcom.net>. Online resources and direct access to over 180 websites.

Leadership University. Accessed at <www.leaderu.com>. One of my favorites! This site is loaded with material, and covers relevant issues pertaining to our culture and our faith. Allow yourself plenty of "surfing" time and enjoy!

Hotlines

CHADD—for children with attention-deficit disorder: 1-800-233-4050.

Clearinghouse on Child Abuse and Neglect Information: 1-800-394-3366.

Family Resources: 1-800-641-4546. This child-abuse prevention agency in Pittsburgh, Pennsylvania has a "WARMLINE" available seven days a week where you can get parenting advice about nonmedical issues.

La Leche League International—counseling for nursing mothers: 1-800-525-3243.

National Child Abuse Hotline, Child Help, USA: 1-800-422-4453. This is an excellent resource for survivors of child abuse and for mothers who fear they may be in danger of abusing their children. Their trained staff will speak with you and provide you with professional referrals for more extensive counseling with a professional in your local area.

National Clearinghouse for Alcohol and Drug Information: 1-800-662-HELP.

National Resource Center on Child Sexual Abuse: 1-800-543-7006.

What Can You Expect?

A Summary of
Child Developmental Stages

The following summary has helped me a great deal to learn what I can reasonably expect from my children. It was taken from an online article by Elaine M. Gibson, "How Kids Grow: Defining Normal Behavior Birth through Age Twelve," found in a series of pages called *The Challenge of Difficult Children: Elaine M. Gibson's Insights on Parenting.* This material may be found at <www.smu.edu/~egibson/development.html> and has been used with permission.

Infancy

What to expect: Near total dependency.

Needs: Love and basic care. Also needed: nutrition, kisses, steady diaper changes, appropriate stimulation, and occasional changes of scenery.

Discipline: Almost none at this stage except for consistency and predictability. A small baby can't be spoiled by too much attention or holding.

Parents' needs: Time off and sleep.

Special problems: Fussiness, diaper rash, feeding problems.

Six Months

What to expect: Child is always moving.

Favorite game: Dropping and throwing toys. Child puts everything into his or her mouth.

Needs: Same as infancy, with added vigilance. Never leave child unattended. Babies roll off beds, changing tables. Unless baby is on the floor, keep a hand on the baby or use a restraint system. Keep small things off the floor and out of reach.

Discipline: Take things away from baby or remove baby from tempting situations. The word "no" should be used in moderation, gently, and with patience. The baby is beginning to understand but has little control over impulses.

Nine Months

What to expect: Baby is crawling, pulling up. Child has no concept of property. Everything is a toy. Still puts everything in mouth.

Needs: Childproof environment. Close supervision.

Discipline: Discipline by moving the child away from the problem or move the problem away from the child. Use the word "no" with kind firmness.

Special problems: Separation fears. Baby is afraid to be left, wakes up during the night.

One Year

What to expect: Child needs to explore and is into everything. Likes to dump things out. Child must touch and taste everything that is new. Likes to tear paper apart and pull plants over to see what will happen. Enjoys throwing food on the floor to see what will happen. Wants to eat what others are eating.

Needs: Lots of hugs, safe environment, firm limits, plenty of sleep, nutritious food.

Discipline: The best discipline is distraction and a firm voice. Physical punishment is not understood by the child. Remove the child from the problem or take the problem away from the child.

Fifteen Months

What to expect: Likes to put things in and take them out again. Wants to feed self but can eat only with fingers. Takes one nap per day, usually in the afternoon. Goes to bed easily. May start biting. Teething pain makes gums sensitive, and biting makes them feel better. Does not understand the word *don't*.

Needs: Close watching, gentle corrections, and encouragement.

Discipline: To stop the child, physically move him. Yelling or hitting won't teach the child "no." Do not expect the child to obey, even though the child understands much of what you say.

Eighteen Months

What to expect: Still into everything. Starts climbing. Needs pull toys and toys to hug and cuddle. Can drink from a cup by himself but spills all the time. Can fill a spoon but cannot turn the handle to get it in the mouth. Refuses to let parents feed him. Easily upset. Wakes during the night. Can remove clothes and shoes and prefers not to be dressed. Often disobeys. Runs away from parents. Starts sit-down temper tantrums. Refuses to cooperate, either by saying "no" or pulling away.

Needs: A few rules are necessary, but the child forgets all the old ones when given a new rule. Use kindness to correct the child or you will have a very anxious or a very naughty three-year-old.

Discipline: To correct him, hold the child's hands, speak clearly, use the same words for each rule. Save spanking for physically dangerous situations; one swat is all that is necessary to get the child's attention. Praise the child when he does things you like.

Twenty-One Months

What to expect: Can handle a cup well but spills all the time. Wants to push the stroller. Likes to run around without shoes or clothes. Can indicate his own needs, behavior starts to get worse. Demands things, *now!* Biting can be a problem.

Needs: Give even more love during bratty stages.

Discipline: Most effective discipline is separation. Remove the child from a bad situation or let the child sit on a time-out chair (four minutes) when the child is naughty. When the child falls apart, put the child to bed.

Special situation: Fussy child, won't eat, sleep, or play? Take the child's temperature. The child is probably sick.

Two Years

What to expect: Likes to remove everything from drawers and cupboards. Can hold a glass with one hand but still has difficulty with a spoon. Is not interested in eating and becomes a poor eater. Dawdles, plays, and refuses to eat at mealtimes. Can help in getting dressed by putting arms and legs in the holes. Asks "What's that?" refers to self by name, and *loves* to say "no." Likes to be outdoors and makes a short walk last a long time. Picks up everything he sees. Under pressure, runs from parents.

May be ready to use a toilet but will not have adequate control for another year. Out-of-control temper tantrums when frustrated or tired—very classic behavior. Calls parents back after put to bed. Needs bedtime rituals in order to go to bed. Makes rituals out of everything. Wants to make own decisions.

Needs: Parents have to be smarter, not tougher or more out of control, than the child is. Child needs limited choices: Either…or. Don't ask if the child wants to do what he or she has to do. Teach the child real names for all the child's body parts.

Discipline: Understand things from the child's viewpoint, then help the child adapt to requirements. Separation (time out) is the best tool. Work on one thing at a time. Don't act like your two-year-old.

Two-and-a-Half

What to expect: This is *the* Age of Conflict. Child is never sure whether he wants to be independent and separate ("Me do it," "myself," "no, no, no") or dependent and treated like a baby ("Hold me," "carry me," "help me"). Parents never know what to expect. Temper tantrums increase and are used for attention and control. Child wants the same foods all the time, refuses any change, says "no" even when she means "yes." May start to stutter or stammer or masturbate frequently. Wants to be treated like a baby when tired. The child is just starting to learn the rules and tells himself "no, no" while breaking them.

Needed: Patient, kind, firm parents.

Discipline: Easy time to overuse spanking, but it will not help: The child's bad behavior will get worse. Instead of spanking all the time, learn to ignore attention-getting misbehavior when possible. Take over for the child when necessary. Separation is useful for both child and parent. Avoid useless power struggles. Parents need time off every day to relax and regain patience. When things get too crazy, parents may need to spend some time alone in the bathroom in order to calm down.

Three

What to expect: Likes to do things by himself. Can unbutton and unzip own clothes. Does not know the front from the back or which shoe fits on which foot and doesn't care. Favorite expression is "all by myself," but cries easily when can't do something. Child wants to help parents do things. May refuse to hold parent's hand. Wants to walk in stores instead of riding in stroller. Develops sudden fears and phobias. Resists taking naps but needs them. Can control bladder and bowel functions but still has accidents. By three and a half, child whines all the time. May stammer and stutter when upset or excited. Nose picking, fingernail biting, and thumb sucking reach a peak. Child also learns to spit. Favorite lines are "Don't look," "Don't laugh," "Don't talk"—which the child uses on parents. Prime time for imaginary friends.

Needs: Patience, time to grow. Remember, a three-year-old is a baby that looks like a child. Don't force threes to be bigger than they can be at the moment. An enabling environment.

Discipline: This child wants to be good. Help her. Tell the child what you expect and why before the child asks and before the child misbehaves. Needs honesty from parents. If the child's mistakes are treated like crimes, child may develop emotional problems. Treat accidents like learning experiences. Show the child how to make amends.

Four

What to expect: The "out of bounds" four is exuberant and rebellious. The child talks well and may think she is a big shot. Fours tell outrageous lies and are very stubborn. They talk all the time and mix reality and fantasy. They ask "why" in order to argue. They are bossy and defiant: "I won't." They refuse to nap but will fall asleep at 5:30, then wake up ready to stay up all night. They think up all sorts of ways to avoid getting in bed. At night, they are likely to have bad dreams. Fours can dress and undress themselves with little assistance. They eat too fast or not at all. They can now wash hands and face and brush teeth without assistance if they have been trained. They run ahead of adults and refuse to hold hands. Fours play "feelies" with other children and need honest information about bodies and babies. A fussy four needs exercise and then a rest. When excited, the child will need to urinate. When stressed, the child's stomach will hurt.

Needs: Social opportunities. Small play groups. Props for pretend play. Art materials for creative expression. Tolerance. Parents with a sense of humor.

Discipline: Don't argue with a four. Talk less than the child does. Asking a four if he or she did something tempts the child to lie. Teach the child the consequences for misbehavior; then when the child misbehaves, apply the consequences. Be very consistent with a four, and the child will learn to control his own behavior. Four seems big, but the child is still a baby when stressed or tired. Give lots of hugs and kisses, even if you have to catch the child to do it.

Five

What to expect: A five can take charge of bathroom responsibilities, wants to tie shoelaces, can dress with skill, cross streets safely, needs to help with the family chores, and cannot be left alone. Investigates everything—including fire. Eats more than ever before. When playing, makes up rules as he or she goes along.

Needs: Lots of sleep (no naps). Good food (no junk). Plenty of exercise (limited TV). Attention for good behavior. Training in cooperation.

Discipline: Privileges need to be connected to responsibilities. Consequences for misbehavior need to be clear before child misbehaves.

Six

What to expect: Is fiercely independent, a real "know it all." Is obsessed with rules. In perpetual motion, especially at the table. Seldom finishes food and has no table manners. Always in motion but clumsy; can run into the wall and trip over her own shadow. A six tattles to let adults know that he knows the rules. May have temper tantrums again. Worst behavior when the child is with mother.

Needs: Responsibility for self-care. Hates to be babied.

Discipline: Sixes are best with the father. It is better to let father take over the difficult times such as meals, bath, and bedtime. Make expectations clear and consistent.

Seven

What to expect: Sevens complain all the time, mostly about parents. At this age, most children decide they are adopted, even if they aren't. All they think about is playing. Feel mistreated by everyone, withdraw from trouble and complain. Do care what others think about them.

Needs: Listen without solving their problems. Encourage problem solving. Don't overreact with a child this age.

Discipline: Firm kindness. Avoid being manipulated. Don't give in to their oversensitive dramatics. Be patient and encourage at every opportunity.

Eight

What to expect: Demands attention from parents but wants parents to think the way the child does. Oversensitive to parental approval or disapproval. Often fights with mother. Sees every situation as black or white, including rules. May have trouble playing with peers. Boys want to play with boys, and girls want to play with girls. May cry when tired and has stomachaches when worried.

Needs: Recognition. Encouragement. Structure. Techniques to reduce stress.

Discipline: Give lots of attention for good behavior. Describe the behavior. Don't argue with an eight. Rules must be consistent.

Nine

What to expect: Fiddles with things and is increasingly awkward. Friends are more important than mother. Rebels against too many directions and direct orders. Thinks all adults are stupid.

Needs: Skills for cooperation. Opportunities to tell herself what to do.

Discipline: Avoid being too bossy with a nine. Encourage independence and cooperation.

Ten

What to expect: The most docile age. Accepts parents' wishes and generally obeys. Learns to disobey in small rebellions: doesn't mind immediately, argues. Sees rules as flexible and makes excuses for all misbehavior. Demands that friends keep promises.

Needs: Space. Opportunities to make decisions. Must be held accountable for the results of choices.

Discipline: Don't argue. Give them room to rebel in safe ways. Enjoy the ten-year-old. It is a golden age.

Eleven–Twelve

What to expect: Peer pressure is intense. Wants guidance from parents but not lectures. Body changes cause embarrassment and self-consciousness. Girls' behavior becomes erratic as hormonal influences take over. Develops strong friendships. Often embarrassed to be seen in public with parents. Child begins to understand how others feel. Wants to make own decisions, choose own friends.

Needs: Listen to this child; teach by example, not lectures. Build a strong relationship based on respect and caring. Spend time together. Don't try to control the pre-teen; control the consequences. Make expectations very clear *before* a situation arises, not after. Give them a major responsibility for some part of family life. Make them feel useful and necessary. Ignore their complaining about chores. Plain, matter-of-fact talks about sexuality, drugs, the future. Use every opportunity that comes up. Ask the questions; don't wait for them to ask you.

Discipline: Give responsibility and let the child learn from consequences. Don't argue. Listen to the child's feelings to keep the lines of communication open. Make as few rules as possible and enforce them consistently.

You can visit Julie Barnhill's website at:
<www.juliebarnhill.com>

If you are interested in having
Julie Ann Barnhill speak at your special
event, please contact:

Speak Up Speaker Services
1614 Edison Shores Place
Port Huron, MI 48060-3374
Voice: 810-982-0898
Fax: 810-987-4163
E-mail: speakupinc@aol.com
Or log on to <www.speakupspeakerservices.com>
for online scheduling.

Hearts at Home

Hearts at Home is a not-for-profit, nondenominational organization committed to affirming the profession of mothering. It was founded in 1993, and today reaches more than 25,000 mothers at home across the U.S. and Canada. Hearts at Home offers annual conferences and several monthly publications designed to meet the needs of mothers at home, and is committed to communicating to women their God-given value.

Hearts at Home
900 W. College Avenue
Normal, IL 61761
Voice: 309-888-6667
Fax: 309-888-4525
Website: www.hearts-at-home.org
E-mail: hearts@dave-world.net

Notes

Chapter 2—Volcanoes 101

1. Descriptions of the kinds of volcanic eruptions are based on Peter Francis, *Volcanoes* (New York: Penguin, 1976), pp. 108-114; and Robert I. Trilling, *Volcanoes,* online ed., United States Geological Survey Publications website at <pubs.usgs.gov/gip/volc>.

2. Bill Stewart, "St. Helens Spreads Death and Destruction," Clark County, Washington, *Columbian,* May 19, 1980, as reprinted on the *Remember Mount Saint Helens* website at<www.remembersthelens.com/remember/spreads.html>.

Chapter 3—Warning Signs

1. University of Illinois Extension, "Intervening in the Anger Cycle," *FamilyWorks: Strategies for Building Stronger Families,* found on the Internet at <www.urbanext.uiuc.edu/familyworks/anger-02.html>.

Chapter 4—Underground Issues

1. Patrick F. Fagan, "The Child Abuse Crisis: The Disintegration of Marriage and the American Community," *Backgrounder*, no. 1115, May 15, 1997.

2. Kerby Anderson, "Time and Busyness," radio talk reprinted online at <www.leaderu.com/orgs/problem/docs/time.html and associate.com/ministry_files/Other_Electronic_Texts/Probe_Ministries/Time_and_Busyness>, originally broadcast 1992.

3. Stuart Sorenson, "Managing Anger," online article in *Mental Health Sanctuary: The Online Resource for Patients, Families, and Professionals in Mental Health* at <www.mhsanctuary.com/articles/anger.htm>, accessed October 2000.

Chapter 5—Volcanic Damage

1. Quoted in Marie Dawson, "Tools to Counter Abuse: Raising Whole, Healthy Children," *Child Abuse Prevention Series,* Parent Soup Library at

   <http://www.parentsoup.com/library/abuse/tools.html>, accessed
   10/3/00.

2. Children Are Worth Saving Community Outreach Program, "What Is
   Child Abuse and Neglect?" at <http:www.geocities.com/~guardianan-
   gels/abuse_neglect.html>, accessed 2/26/00.

3. Dennis L. Finnan, "Dare to Discipline," *The World and You* radio talk #1297,
   broadcast March 23, 1997, published on *The World and You* website at
   <http://www.wwy.org/wwy1297.html>. The quote within the quote is
   attributed to Russ Walton, *A Handbook to Biblical Solutions* (Brentwood,
   TN: Wolgemuth & Hyatt, 1988).

4. Dennis L. Finnan, "Dare to Discipline."

5. Gary Chapman, "There Must be a Purpose for Anger," *Dr. Chapman's
   Daily Topics,* featured in ViaFamily Internet service at <http://www.
   viafamily.com/chapman/week38day1.html>, adapted from *The Other
   Side of Love: Healing Anger in a Godly Way* (Chicago: Moody Press,
   1999).

Chapter 6—The Bedrock of Truth

1. *Vine's Expository Dictionary of New Testament Words,* "Renew, Renewing,"
   pp. 278-79.

2. "Letters," *Time,* December 8, 1997.

3. "Expenditures on Children by Families," 1999 Annual Report, U.S.
   Department of Agriculture Center for Nutrition Policy and Promo-
   tion, Miscellaneous Publication No. 1528-1999.

Chapter 7—Keeping Things Cool

1. "Managing Your Anger," *Your Family/Health* at WZZK.com. Web
   address: <www.wzzk.com/shared/health/advice/anger11.html>.

2. Charles Swindoll, *The Strong Family: Growing Wise in Family Life* (Portland, OR: Multnomah Press, 1991), p. 61.

3. Swindoll, *The Strong Family,* pp. 63-64.

4. Robert Bianco, "Everybody Loves Patricia," *Minneapolis Star-Tribune,*
   March 16, 1998.

5. Matthew Henry, *Complete Commentary on the Whole Bible,* originally pub-
   lished 1706, reprinted online at *Crosswalk.com:* <bible.crosswalk.com/
   Commentaries/MatthewHenryComplete/mhc-com>, commentary on
   Proverbs 25:28, accessed January, 2000.